Tarek Mitri, ed

Religion, Law and Society

A Christian-Muslim Discussion

WCC Publications, Geneva
Kok Pharos Publishing Co., Kampen

Cover illustration: A calligraphy from an Arab Christian manuscript of 1844. Copyist/artist: Qusṭantīn Dāud al-Ḥumsī. Reproduced by courtesy of the Antiochian Orthodox Study Centre, University of Balamand, Lebanon. The text is from Psalms 119:1:

Blessed are those whose ways are blameless,
who walk according to the law of the Lord.

Ṭubāhum Alladhīn Bilā 'Ayb
fī Tarīqihim al Sālikūn fī Nāmūs al Rabb Da' iman

Cover design: Edwin Hassink

ISBN 2-8254-1148-5 (WCC)
ISBN 90-390-0514-1 (Kok Pharos)

Printed in Switzerland

Religion, Law and Society

Contents

Introduction *Tarek Mitri* vii

Part I

1. Typologies of Religion and State *Sheila McDonough* 1

Part II

2. *Sharīʻah* and Modernity *Walid Saif* 11
3. The Implications of *Sharīʻah*, *Fiqh* and *Qānūn* in an Islamic State *Tayyib Z. Al-Abdin* 20
4. *Sharīʻah*, Change and Plural Societies *Jørgen S. Nielsen* . . 27
5. *Tashrīʻ* (Process of Law-Making) in Islam *Asghar Ali Engineer* 33
6. Notes on *Sharīʻah*, *Fiqh* and *Ijtihād* *Mokhtar Ihsan Aziz* . . 44
7. On the Urgency of *Ijtihād* *Khalid Ziadeh* 48

Part III

8. *Sharīʻah* and Religious Pluralism *Bert F. Breiner* 51
9. Islamic *Sharīʻah* and the Status of Non-Muslims *Ghazi Salahuddin Atabani* 63
10. Muslim Minorities and *Sharīʻah* in Europe *Gé Speelman* . . 70

Part IV

11. Secularism and Religion *Mohammed Ben-Yunusa* 78

12. Religion and Secularization: Introductory Remarks from a Western-Christian Perspective *Heinz Klautke* 86

13. Secularism and Religion: Alternative Bases for the Quest for a Genuine Pluralism *Bert F. Breiner* 92

14. State, Religion and Laïcité: The Western European Experience *Jørgen S. Nielsen* 100

15. The Role of Religious Institutions and *'ulamā'* in a Contemporary Muslim Society *Tayyib Z. Al-Abdin* 111

Part V

16. Human Rights and Islamic Revivalism *Walid Saif* 119

17. Differing Perceptions of Human Rights: Asian-African Interventions at the Human Rights Conference *Thomas Michel* . 131

Contributors 138

Introduction

TAREK MITRI

Calls for the implementation of Islamic law (*taṭbīq al-Shari'ah*) or attempts to impose it are generally met among Christians with fear, indignation and protest. The major preoccupation of those who live in predominantly Muslim countries often centres on their civil and political rights as members of religious minorities. Though assured that their basic religious freedom is guaranteed and their personal laws recognized, they perceive the enforcement of *Sharī'ah* as leading to their marginalization and even subordination. This preoccupation is echoed in the more widespread opinion that invoking legal systems elaborated in historical circumstances different from those of our present world is a form of retrogression. Also radically questioned is the immutable and normative character of what is seen as a rigid body of law. Whether attributed to the Islamic worldview or to its Islamist interpretation, *Sharī'ah* is depicted as incompatible with modernity and more particularly with what is seen as one of its greatest achievements: the Universal Declaration of Human Rights.

A no less critical approach points to the inadequacy of a religiously based alternative to positive law and to the claim that it provides in itself a radical solution to present-day political, social, economic and cultural problems.

It is not surprising, therefore, that the suggestion of a constructive dialogue with proponents of *Sharī'ah*, which goes beyond stating disagreements or expressing discontent, is often dismissed as unrealistic and at worst hazardous.

The passionate convictions of many Islamists, the sensationalist perceptions of their detractors and the anxieties of those who face a real or potential threat do not favour dialogue. Indeed, what is seen as the imposition of an all-embracing juridical, social and political order, neither founded on popular consent nor based on a social contract, seems to exclude the minimal conditions for a fair dialogue. Yet it should also be added that convictions held with equal passion by many Christians are not unrelated to their own reluctance to risk dialogue: to portray the call for the implementation of *Sharī'ah* as reactionary and obscurantist and secularization as an irreversible socio-historical process leaves little space for a serious consideration of Islamist discourse.

Despite these obstacles and limitations, dialogue remains possible and, in the view of those who are aware of its potential, desirable. Without having any illusions about changing the course of events rapidly and effectively, dialogue stands as an alternative to war. Clarifying disagreements on this thorny issue is no doubt necessary. Yet discerning elements of convergence and exploring practical — if partial — solutions cannot be dismissed out of hand. The spirit of authentic dialogue is betrayed both by concealing and by absolutizing divergences.

* * *

What has been called the resurgence of political Islam or the re-politicization of Islam points first and foremost to the exacerbation of the crisis of legitimacy in various Arab and Muslim nation-states. It is asserted that the *Ummah* was divided and that this division is inextricably linked with its weakness. The existing entities are creations of colonial rule; and ever since the abolition of the caliphate in 1923 it is widely recognized, in words if not in deeds, that the search for an uncontested legitimacy entails a call for a broader unity.[1] Moreover, Islam has undoubtedly been the underlying cultural basis of the worldview of Muslims, even of pan-Arab secularists, including a number of Christians.

The second facet of the crisis is mirrored in the failure of political systems to achieve the aims from which they derived their own "legitimacy". They did not remain — and some were not from the beginning — expressions of popular consent. Rather, they developed into self-proclaimed agents of independence, liberation and social justice.

The concern for legitimacy (*shar'iyyah*) in Islamist thought is inevitably linked with the implementation of Islamic law. Exercising politics in conformity with the law (*al siyāsa al shar'iyyah*, as Ibn Taymiyyah puts it in the title of one of his books) is the primary criterion of legitimate government. This is perhaps best illustrated by the formula *lā shar'iyyah bi ghayr shari'ah* (no legitimacy without Islamic law).[2] The call for the implementation of Islamic law also functions as an affirmation of authenticity (*aṣālah*) against those who claimed authenticity while adopting "imported" legal systems.

All this indicates how *Sharī'ah*, while perceived as a solution, or an alternative prompted by "necessity", remains above all an "obligation".[3] To many Muslims the reference to obligation, powerfully advocated, opens the way for the "voices of millenarian dreams" to surpass those of historical criticism and self-criticism.[4] Sustained by varying degrees of religious fervour, it proves effective as a vehicle of political mobilization. Uncompromising in its very nature, it does not invest much effort in articulating how it is responsive to "necessity", assuming that the latter conveys a meaning complementary to religious duty.

The call for the implementation of *Sharī'ah*, whether it appeals for the restoration of the model of society shaped by the Prophet Muḥammad in Al Madīnah or invites a reconstruction of this model, does not necessarily propose a homogeneous, well-defined and delimited body of legal texts. It is thus fair to say that the Islamists, even if politically successful, will not find an agreed upon and coherent system they can immediately apply.

Nevertheless, they argue that *Sharī'ah* is all-encompassing and provides elaborated solutions to many present problems, while others will have to be solved in accordance with a set of rules, of which analogy (*qiyās*) is the most universally accepted. In this connection, a number of applications of *Sharī'ah* occupy a more noteworthy place in their teachings and advocacy. A case in point is the punishment laws or penal prescriptions (*al ḥudūd*), highlighted and exaggerated by sensational actions and no less sensationalist coverage in the media, and feared by Christian minorities.

A wide-embracing understanding of *Sharī'ah* is also common among Muslims who do not share the Islamists' viewpoint. But their understanding involves a different approach — one which distinguishes between the normative and the contextual, insists on returning to the Qur'ān itself and differentiates between *Sharī'ah* and *fiqh* (jurisprudence).

It would be unfair and unwise to ignore the contribution of those who seem to follow a *via media* between the Islamists and the secularists and to overlook the significance of intra-Muslim dialogue and its real and potential consequences. Like all genuine dialogue, it strives to go beyond mutual anathemas, exclusion and reductionism. A relevant Christian-Muslim dialogue on *Sharī'ah* cannot progress, or even occur, except in relation to the exchanges and debates among Muslims.

This sensitivity can open up a space for a fruitful reflection, which will not only remove misunderstandings and subsequently recognize and respect differences, but also embark upon reciprocal questioning. It is worth noting that such an effort of sharpening definitions, drawing distinctions and suggesting clarifications has not been overlooked by concerned religious leaders, intellectuals and political activists.[5] But this should extend well beyond a limited circle and address as well the concrete problems at stake in various national contexts.

* * *

The term *Sharīʻah*, found only once in the Qur'ān, originally means "the right way".[6] It thus conveys an inclusive sense. Somewhat less inclusive are two other Quranic references, in which derivatives of this word seem to acquire a more directive (*sharraʻa lakum*) or legal (*shirʻa-tan*) connotation.[7] In the course of Islamic history, *Sharīʻah* came to cover all Islamic precepts, both "religious" and "legal". While recognizing this historical fact, however, theologians and jurists did not necessarily agree on a common approach to the rich and diverse body of literature called *fiqh* or jurisprudence, the theory and codification of *Sharīʻah*. All affirmed the centrality of "going back" to the Quranic text and the recorded practices of the Prophet and his companions. But there are differing opinions on the normativity of *fiqh* and on identifying what is more specifically "binding" throughout its historical development. The complex discussions about the "established" schools of law (*Madhāhib*) and their definitive status and about the rigidity of the applications of *fiqh* rules are beyond the scope of this introduction. We simply note that Islamists themselves affirm, sometimes in different ways, that implementing *Sharīʻah* does not entail elevating *fiqh* to a comparable status. Yet their critics could not help observing that they did not systematically make the necessary distinctions or avoid the temptation of confusing *Sharīʻah* with its *fiqh* applications — or rather some of them, chosen at the expense of others.

It is probably more appropriate for our purposes to single out the position of those who, as they emphasize the primacy of *Sharīʻah*, consider the *fiqh* rules open to a new *ijtihād* (literally, effort or struggle) and do not hesitate to draw with a measure of freedom on the great variety within the historical legacy of interpretation. The criterion to be used in this effort lies in the assertion that the aims of *Sharīʻah* (*maqāṣid al-sharīʻah*) constitute the frame of reference according to which practical implementation is to be measured.[8] If the general purposes of *Sharīʻah*, such as justice, equality and the welfare of the community, are constant, the concrete and specific implementations are circumstantial or situational. What are referred to in *Sharīʻah* terminology as *al maṣāliḥ al mursalah* ("the open common interests") are to be considered a major source for laws that meet new needs. It goes without saying that examining standing interests and exploring adequate legal prescriptions require a collective search that could not be restricted to jurists. Such an activity could lead to the reconsideration of certain traditionally accepted laws that prove incompatible with present estimates of the interests of the society. Another criterion is derived from the principle that "necessities permit what is otherwise prohibited" (*al ḍarūrāt tubīh al-maḥẓūrāt*). This principle is in turn closely connected to another *Sharīʻah* rule, which states that "no practice should cause damage to oneself or to others" (*lā ḍarūrah wa lā ḍarār*), which is complemented by the principle that "avoiding damage and harm overrides acquiring benefits" (*dar'u al-mafāsid khayrun min jalb al-manāfi'*).

Emphasis on the aims of *Sharīʻah* and an invitation to the creative understanding of its implementation could make it possible to address some of the most controversial issues in a less simplistic or reductionist manner than many Islamists and their opponents are prepared to follow. A case in point — which often overshadows other important issues — is the question of punishment laws. When, under what conditions and how they should be dealt with deserve more attention than passionate polarization allows for. It is not unfounded in *fiqh* to say that an Islamic state should not claim their immediate and scrupulous enforcement until it has fulfilled its obligations towards the community of ensuring social justice and civil rights. Moreover, if punishment proves to be an urgency prompted by the collective interests in a specific context, a number of conditions ought seriously to be taken into account. A general rule stipulates that "punishments are precluded by doubts and suspicions" (*tudra' al ḥudūd bil shubuhāt*). An additional limitation to their strict enforcement rests in the invitation to repentance and in the responsibility of persuasion and guidance.

Another thorny issue is that of the rights of non-Muslims in an Islamic state. The *dhimmi* condition, praised by many Islamists as synonymous with justice and minority protection and depicted by their critics as a codified form of subordination, is re-examined by those who, in view of the principles described above, attempt to reconcile *Sharīʻah* with the modern reality of citizenship. The unanimously cited guiding affirmation found in the *Ḥadīth*, "to them belongs whatever belongs to us and incumbent upon them is whatever is incumbent upon us" (*lahum mā lanā wa 'alayhum mā 'alaynā*), is seen not as an apology but rather as an invitation to look afresh at the question of civil and political equality. Some have cautiously suggested that justice be considered a more appropriate notion, while "classification" of "citizens" as Muslims and non-Muslims not be equated with "discrimination".[9]

Beyond these somewhat subtle distinctions, reflecting the difference between community and nation, others echo the saying of the Prophet Muḥammad in Al Madīnah that Muslims and non-Muslims are *ummattun wāḥidatun* (one people). Seen against the background of full participation of non-Muslims in national life, this affirmation gains a new significance in present times and calls for a revision of rights and obligations of those who have been traditionally called *dhimmiyīn* and ought now to be treated as co-citizens. A number of Muslim thinkers legitimate this new outlook by defining the *dhimmah* pact as an historical "contract" rather than the consecration of a permanent status of inferiority.[10]

It would however be unjustified to assume that the problem is thus solved once and for all. Reconciling the aims of *Sharī'ah* in the realm of justice with the Quranic text and *Ḥadīth* remains an unfinished task. Despite the emphasis on not doing any injustice, the Quranic verse referring to *dhimmiyīn* being humiliated or "brought low"[11] and the *Ḥadīth* stating that "Islam rules and is not ruled" cannot be bypassed, even if some reinterpretation has been attempted.[12]

* * *

A Christian-Muslim dialogue on *dhimmah*, crucial as it is, cannot progress if undertaken exclusively or in isolation from some of the broader issues we have discussed. Nor could it bear fruit if caught in the confrontation between the dogmatic secularism that Christians are presumed to herald and the call to the restoration of theocracy which is attributed to Muslims.[13] The notion, still current, that the Muslim community cannot admit any distinction between temporal power and religious authority does not withstand careful scrutiny. Nor can we bind a Christian worldview to the assertion that religion is an entirely private affair or a spiritual matter *strictu sensu*. In two different ways both Islam and Christianity bear witness that the truths of revelation relate to life in society and to the legitimacy and responsibilities of governments. The whole realm of the state cannot be immunized from the significance of religion. Moreover, the relationship between religion and politics is not to be tackled in a way that projects the European historical experience onto the realities of the Muslim world. For Christians living in predominantly Muslim societies a change of perspective about the place of Islamic law might be necessary. It deserves to be regarded at least as a heritage, certainly no less worthy of recognition than Roman law and its modern derivatives. This would in turn invite Muslims to be more attentive to the historicity of legal systems. Without departing from their faith and their understanding of revelation as a source and guarantee of law, they may accept the drawing of a distinction between principles and applications.[14] In addition, Christians and Muslims may be able to agree that the respective autonomy of state and religion could be realized without requiring privatization of the latter or separating religion from society.[15]

Christians, whether living in Islamic societies or not, cannot engage in a constructive dialogue with Muslims on *Sharī'ah* without rethinking their rather negative view of law, which they often oppose to "grace" or "love". The "Pharisaic image" or discontent with the "Constantinian compromise" which are associated with this view should not prevent a re-examination of the public role of religion. Christians do face, in their own terms, the challenge to which Muslims try to respond in seeing *Sharī'ah* as preoccupied with the wholeness of life, private and public.

There is no doubt that the call for the implementation of *Sharī'ah* generates many problems. The urgency of these problems and the need to address them concretely in the various national contexts cannot be minimized, let alone overlooked, by a genuine desire for reflection and exchange of ideas. But we cannot afford to regard this task as secondary or marginal nor dismiss its relevance to us and to peaceful and harmonious living with our neighbours.

* * *

This book is the fruit of two Christian-Muslim colloquia convened by the Office on Interreligious Relations of the World Council of Churches. They were motivated by a desire to concentrate on the most timely and controversial issues outlined in the "Ecumenical Considerations" on issues in Christian-Muslim relations which were received by the WCC Central Committee in 1992.[16]

Held in Switzerland (Geneva and Nyon) in December 1992 and November 1993, these colloquia discussed "Religion, Law and Society" in an attempt to broaden the scope of dialogue on *Sharī'ah*. Christians and Muslims were invited to re-examine the complex relation of their religions to society and state. The participants were well aware of the many obstacles to a genuine dialogue. Many Christians do often think that Islam, in its claim to embrace all aspects of life, favours a "theocratic" model similar to that which is familiar from the history of Christendom. Many Muslims, on the other hand, are inclined to suggest that Christians today have been led, through a socio-historical process which has been resisted but ultimately accepted, to reduce their religion to a strictly spiritual and private affair. The former position fails to recognize that religious authority and political power need not be amalgamated in Islam. While it is true that power historically sought a religious legitimacy, it nevertheless functioned according to a somewhat "secular" model. The latter position likewise falls short in failing to admit that Christian faith cannot be isolated from the realms of society and politics.

Such a general clarification, needless to say, was far from closing the debate. A typology of religion-state relations introduced the first colloquium into an historicized comparative approach. Another introduction, it was felt, was indispensable. Notions of *fiqh* and law had to be differentiated from *Sharī'ah* before addressing it from the perspectives of the rights of non-Muslims, human rights and modernity.

The "theoretical" dialogue, as demanding and crucial as it is, could not overshadow the present concrete situations in the Muslim world and the West. The case of Sudan, as a country in which an Islamic model of society and governance is proposed, was discussed at some length, opening up the debate on power-sharing in plural societies and on legal pluralism. The situation of Muslim minorities in Europe and the challenges of secular societies mirrored the other facet of the same questions.

The unfinished dialogue agenda was carried forward to the second colloquium. The issues of secularization, legal pluralism, the role of religious institutions, theologians and *'ulamā'* and human rights were discussed. Elements of convergence were not stated as affirmations but rather implied in a set of questions.

Participants asked whether resistance to secularism as an ideology entails a reluctance to confront the challenges of secularization. They also asked how "creative interaction" between "the processes of this world" and "the fundamental resources of belief" could be made possible, so that Christians and Muslims might "exert a legitimate influence in the public domain".

It was noted that legal pluralism remains an area of controversy. The nation-state model, rejected in many ways among Muslims, implies a common legal system, while the model derived from *Sharī'ah* allows for legal pluralism. Could pluralism be safeguarded without a system of shared values? Can both faiths find expression in legal concepts and structures that bind society together rather than split it apart?

With respect to religious institutions and leaders, it was recognized that some serve and others challenge the prevailing cultural and political power systems. How can these institutions free themselves to impart a universal perspective on contemporary issues? How can clergy be trained to use the best of both faith traditions, learning from the achievements of the natural and social sciences?

Regarding human rights, the discussion took a practical course. While it was suggested that they be taken up as the focus of a continued Christian-Muslim dialogue, ways and means of interreligious cooperation were explored. How do people of faith defend human dignity independently of special interests or cultural and political centres of power? How do Christians and Muslims find together a balance between the rights of individuals and those of communities? In what ways is it possible to develop together concepts, or even a language, in the field of human rights rooted in the common core values of the two religions?

The agenda of "Religion, Law and Society" is thus not exhausted. It is hoped that such an unprecedented Christian-Muslim discussion, initiated by the WCC, will enrich and stimulate the much-needed dialogue at the national level.

NOTES

1 The unity of "the Arab world" and that of "the abode of Islam" do not coincide in terms of their political and geographical scope. The former implies a more or less secular meaning of "nation". However, the use of the same term — *Ummah* — has tended to confuse the religious notion of the political community established by the Prophet Muḥammad with the notion espoused by modern nationalism.

2 Cf. Ali Garisha and Muhammad Sharif Zaybaq, *Asālīb al Ghazw al Fikrī lil ʿĀlam al-Islāmī* ("The ways of intellectual invasion in the Muslim world"), Cairo, 1978.

3 A major book by one of the most prominent Islamist intellectuals, Shaykh Yusuf al-Qarḍāwī, is entitled *Al Ḥall al-Islāmī Farīḍah wa Ḍarūrah* ("The Islamic solution is an obligation and a necessity"), Beirut, 1975.

4 Bassam Tibi, "Arabic Literature of Islamic Revivalism", in *Islam and Christian-Muslim Relations* Vol. 3, no. 2, Dec. 1992, p.189.

5 This is illustrated by two colloquia that brought together Islamist and "nationalist" Arab intellectuals, including Christians. Cf. *Al Ṣaḥwah al Islāmiyyah wa Humūm al Waṭan al ʿArabī* ("The Islamic awakening and the preoccupation of the Arab nation"), Amman, Arab Thought Forum, 1987; and *Al Ḥiwar al-Qawmī al-Dīnī* ("The nationalist-religious dialogue"), Cairo, Centre of Arab Unity Studies, 1989.

6 "Then we put thee on the right Way of Religion: so follow", Sūrat al-Jāthiyah (kneeling) (45:18). This and other Quranic verses quoted in this introduction are from the translation of A. Yusuf Ali, Beirut, Dar al ʻArabiyyah, 1968.

7 "The same religion has He established for you", Sūrat al-Shūra (consultation) (42:13); "to each among you have we prescribed a Law and an open way", Sūrat al-Māʼidah (the table spread) (5:48).

8 See the paper by Walid Saif, "Sharīʻah and Modernity", pp.11-19.

9 See Fahmī Huwaydī, "Al Saḥwah al Islāmiyyah wa al Muwāṭanah wa al Musāwāt ("The Islamic awakening, citizenship and equality") in *Al Ṣaḥwah al Islāmiyyah wa Humūm al Waṭan ʻal Arabī.*

10 See Aḥmad Kamal Abu al-Majd, "Hawl al-Daʻwah ila Ṭaṭbīq al-Shariʻah al-Islāmiyyah" ("Concerning the call to the implementation of Islamic *Sharīʻah*"), in *Al Ḥiwar al-Qawmī al-Dīnī.*

11 Sūrat al-Tawbah (repentance) (9:29).

12 There are Ḥanafī jurists who suggest that implementing *Sharīʻah* on someone who does not believe in it means humiliation; cf. Radwan al Sayyed, "Al Masīḥiyyūn fī al fiqh al Islāmī", ("Christians in Islamic jurisprudence"), in *Al Masīḥiyyūn al ʻArab* ("The Arab Christians"), Beirut, 1981, p.52.

13 The call for the implementation of *Sharīʻah* and the "return" to theocracy are not to be equated, according to most Islamists. They insist that the concept of the "rule of God" *(ḥākimiyyat Allah)* does not propose a political model comparable to the theocratic one known in the history of Christianity. More clarity on this question should be sought in dialogue.

14 See Youakim Moubarrac, "Approches chrétiennes de l'Islam", in *Islam et Christianisme en dialogue*, Paris, Edition du Cerf, 1982, pp.133f.

15 Groupe de Recherches Islamo-Chrétien (GRIC), "Etat et religion", *Islamochristiana*, no. 12, Rome, 1986, pp.49-72.

16 *Issues in Christian-Muslim Relations: Ecumenical Considerations*, Geneva, WCC, 1992. This document was drafted in the light of the *Guidelines on Dialogue with People of Living Faiths*, received by the WCC Central Committee in 1979 and sent to churches "for their consideration and discussion, animated testing and evaluation, and for their elaboration in each specific situation". Widely circulated, these *Guidelines* have been reprinted in 1982, 1984, 1990 and 1993.

Part I

1. Typologies of Religion and State

SHEILA MCDONOUGH

A short paper presenting a typology of religion and state relationships in the Christian and Islamic traditions can do no more than point to a few interpretative keys that may help to understand the two traditions, both of which have long and complex histories. For the most part, however, Christians and Muslims have very little knowledge about each other's history. This mutual ignorance is no accident. Norman Daniel has persuasively argued that Christians refused for centuries to look seriously at Islam.[1] The converse is also true, although perhaps for different reasons. One may hope that this period of mutual ignorance is coming to an end; and if no one can predict how Christians and Muslims will view each other when both have digested much more information about the historical record of the other, one can nevertheless reasonably suggest that mutual knowledge can at least eliminate much of the current unjust stereotyping.

Typologies are always abstractions, lifted out of historical reality in order to illuminate a point. The historical reality is always much more complex than the typology might suggest. Typologies are tools to be used in interpretation; they can help to give a perspective and shed some light on particular historical contexts, but no typology represents the whole of any actual historical situation.

The Christian and Islamic traditions both understand themselves as heirs of the tradition of Abraham, and we may begin by looking at passages mentioning Abraham in the New Testament and the Qur'ān which could be understood as having implications for religion and the state. From the New Testament:

> His mercy is for those who fear him
>   from generation to generation.
> He has shown strength with his arm;
>   he has scattered the proud in the thoughts of their hearts.

He has brought down the powerful from their thrones,
and lifted up the lowly;
he has filled the hungry with good things,
and sent the rich away empty...
in remembrance of his mercy...
to Abraham and to his descendants forever (Luke 1:50-55).

From the Qur'ān:

And remember that Abraham
Was tried by his Lord
With certain Commands,
Which he fulfilled;
He said: "I will make thee
An Imām to the Nations."
He pleaded: "And also [Imāms]
from my offspring!"
He answered: "But My Promise
Is not within the reach of evildoers..."

And remember Abraham said:
"My Lord, make this a City
of Peace! and feed its People
with fruits! — such of them
As believe in Allah and the Last Day" (2:124-126).

As these passages indicate, both traditions begin with the understanding of a promise from a merciful God that good people will be helped. In each case, this help is related to the understanding that the people will live in expectation of God's judgment on their finite efforts; and this judgment is expected both within and beyond the experiences of history.

While it is not easy to measure the impact of passages like these on actual historical situations, both these images of Abraham resonate in our century as sources of inspiration for various Christian and Muslim individuals and groups working and hoping for a better future. Both traditions carry within their scriptures images of renewal; and many times in their respective histories these images have served to generate new beginnings and new hopes.

Protesting and ordering

Two key images in both traditions are "protesting" and "ordering". The former presents an imperative to believers to protest against perceived forms of corruption and injustice; the latter encourages them to create social and political structures which can serve to ward off chaos and to maintain ordered and stable forms of corporate existence. The two perspectives exist in tension within both traditions, with sometimes one, sometimes the other playing a more dominant role.

In the Christian case, the initial three centuries of Christian history are generally understood as a "protesting" phase, when the new community was struggling to survive in the pagan milieu of the Roman empire. The protesting in many cases meant cruel martyrdom at the hands of the Romans. The "ordering" phase came after the Emperor Constantine was converted to Christianity in 312 CE,[2] and from the fourth to the sixteenth century of Christian history the ordering image was the dominant one.

In the Muslim case, the original Makkah period of the Prophet's life might be viewed as the "protesting" phase, and the Al Madīnah period as the model of the "ordering" phase. From this perspective, subsequent Muslim history until the eighteenth century CE might be considered the ordering phase.[3]

The use of such typologies does not imply that the "protesting" and "ordering" phases of the two communities were identical in every respect; rather, it means that such a comparison may helpfully illuminate certain similar characteristics in the two communities. Constantine has sometimes been compared to Mu'āwiyah as an indication of a kind of decline in the idealism of the earlier period. But whether one compares Constantine to the Prophet in Al Madīnah or to Mu'āwiyah, one is in each case just using an abstract typology which might indicate something about the actual historical situation. The typology could be used to illuminate something about both cases without necessarily implying contradiction or inconsistency. Typologies are like coloured glasses used to look at the historical data to see if new insights can thus be gained. In other words, one asks different sorts of questions depending on which typology is guiding the questioning.

If one phase of the history of a tradition is said to be directed more towards "protesting" and another towards "ordering", it does not mean that all the activities and attitudes within that phase are of the one type. In any actual historical situation, aspects of both protesting and ordering will be at work. But the mix is different at different times and in different places. There are of course significant differences between the situation of the Emperor Constantine and the Prophet Muḥammad in Al Madīnah. The latter was not an emperor, and he was still receiving revelation. What the two historical situations have in common is a final triumph over paganism.

The Christians of the first three centuries who endured persecution at the hands of pagan Roman emperors paved the way in many respects for the success of the Christian emperor. Once Christianity was established as the official religion of the empire, the torture of the Roman arena was abolished, and more merciful treatment of human beings was instituted in much of political and social life. This is not to say that the rule of Constantine constituted an ideal Christian society. He was an emperor ruling by the force of his command over the Roman army, and most of his people were still not Christians. Nevertheless, his rule began the phase of Christianity as the dominant religion of the state and ended the association of political power with the pagan gods. Never again in the Christian world could an emperor succeed in claiming to be divine.

In the Islamic case, the Prophet Muḥammad finally triumphed over the forces of political power associated with pagan gods when he returned to Makkah at the end of his life. This aspect of his career is comparable to Constantine's victory. There are also many differences between the two cases, the most significant being that the rule of the Prophet is much more considered the source of a normative ideal than was the case with Constantine. Here I simply want to draw attention to the ending of pagan dominance in both cases. Also, the Muslims' endurance of persecution in the "protesting" phase in Makkah might usefully be compared to that of the persecuted Christians in the "protesting" phase of their first three centuries. In both cases, the "protesting" phase seems to be the foundation for the later "ordering" phase.

The comparison mentioned earlier between Constantine and Mu'āwiyah involves the use of a different set of coloured glasses (typology) which also throws some light on the data. Twentieth-century criticism of the two rulers usually characterizes them as monarchs dependent on military power rather than the consent of the people to maintain their rule. Some contemporary Christian thinkers argue that rejecting the Constantinian model is a positive step for the present and future because Christians should see themselves as servants of God, rather than as domineering lords. Many twentieth-century Muslims are similarly critical of Mu'āwiyah as one who somehow weakened the original egalitarian basis of the Muslim community by transforming it into a kind of authoritarian system based on the models of earlier empires.

It is undoubtedly true that both Christian and Muslim civilizations after Constantine and Mu'āwiyah were shaped by authoritarian models of political dominance based on control of military power, and subsequent leaders followed the general patterns established by the authoritarian rulers. On the other hand, paganism was finished as a dominant form of politico-religious life in both cases, and the new forms of religious life and practice among the people were sustained. Neither Constantine nor Mu'āwiyah represented the exemplary ideal of his particular tradition, yet each managed to order and sustain a form of political and social organization in which religious life flourished.

We should also note that the "protesting" aspect of each tradition remained alive and active even in the phase of dominant "ordering" through authoritarian military rule. In the case of Islam, the collecting of *Ḥadīth* and the elaborating of the schools of religious jurisprudence in the ninth century were in the first instance "protesting" forms of activity, since they were directed towards reform of the existing order.[4] In the mediaeval Christian world, numerous types of "protesting" against the established order took place in the name of reform towards a better expression of Christian ideals. The concerns of St Francis for the well-being of all would be one example.

In Christian history, a significant and dramatic change from the model of Constantine was symbolized by the storming of the Bastille in Paris at the end of the eighteenth century. What actually happened to Western society as a result of the revolutions in which the kings of France and England, the German kaiser and Russian czar were rudely brought down from their positions of dominance was that the political structure based on one all-powerful ruler, which Constantine had adopted from his Roman predecessors, was finally abandoned. That revolution also began to have an impact on the Ottoman, Safavid and Moghul empires.[5] If we think of the Ottoman caliph and Persian and Moghul emperors as heirs to the political model of Mu'āwiyah, we note that these rulers eventually disappeared from the pages of history, just like the Christian heirs to the model of Constantine. These events involved massive disturbances of common life and confusion and suffering on a large scale, but one fruit of all the disturbance was the ending of a type of society in which a single ruler, backed up by military power, imposed obedience and conformity on a whole civilization.

To summarize: the Christian and Muslim communities both cherish a trust that God will help good people to build good societies. Both communities lived for centuries, following the models of Constantine and Mu'āwiyah, under systems of authoritarian domination legitimated by acceptance of an established religion. Since the French revolution, the authoritarian systems have collapsed, and both communities are struggling to discover new forms of social order which will enable the people to implement more effectively the ideals latent within their respective traditions. Both communities are presently experimenting with new ways to implement the values of their respective traditions in the context of the changes resulting from the end of the two types of mediaeval social order. Other essays in this volume treat Islamic responses to this challenge; the rest of this paper will focus on some Christian responses to the changes brought about by the French revolution.

The experience of the French revolution

Did Christian societies revert to paganism following the French revolution? The most lucid Christian writer I know on this question is Alexis de Tocqueville, a Roman Catholic member of the French nobility who lived through the French revolution and observed at first hand the destruction of the social world he knew. He then travelled to see the new social and political order which had just been implemented in North America and wrote a book entitled *Democracy in America*, describing and analyzing what he perceived as the probable strengths and weaknesses of this interesting new invention. Most scholars consider his work a remarkably perceptive interpretation of a world that was largely new to him. His motive in writing was to help the French people think through this new experiment and to decide how much or how little to use for themselves.

De Tocqueville thought the Americans were right to have disestablished religion, since his own experience had shown him that, if political power is legitimated by religious authorities and church and state are perceived as supporting and upholding each other, then when the people turn against the state, as they did in the French revolution, they will probably also turn against the religion.[6] Indeed, many Christian priests were killed or exiled during the French revolution precisely because they were perceived as supporters of the king. There is little doubt that the bitterness against Christianity of many of the revolutionaries grew out of their perception of an alliance between religion and the monarchical state.

De Tocqueville also recognized that political power in the new system would be legitimated not by military power but through the consent of the governed expressed in elections. This placed a serious responsibility on the citizens, and free and diligent newspapers would be essential for informing them well on the issues on which they were voting. Under this system, De Tocqueville was certain that there would be continuous changes in the personnel running the government, since the people would regularly want to replace one governing group with another. Consequently, he argued, the religious authorities must keep out of the political arena, so that they would not be thrown out when the people got ready to throw out another government.

In essence, this type of system means that the political leaders may not use force to compel citizens to agree with all their ideas and policies. They must win consent in a non-violent manner, and they often fail to do so.

Secularism takes diverse forms in contemporary Western societies, but the underlying notion is that perceived by de Tocqueville, namely that a government which changes often should not be legitimated by religious authority. People ought to be able to change their political leaders without changing or interfering with their religious lives. Most Christians have agreed with this premise.

De Tocqueville believed that the church would survive better if it were disestablished, since religious leaders would not then be blamed for the wrongdoing of the politicians. The two main points of the US constitution in this regard are that no discrimination with respect to citizens' rights and duties should be made on religious grounds and that the state should not interfere with religion. De Tocqueville and others would say this leaves the churches free to get on with their proper functions. Having personally observed the French revolution trying to destroy Christianity, he believed that the new American system made the survival of the Christian religion more feasible. Later the Russian and Chinese revolutions also tried to abolish traditional religious institutions, further evidence for de Tocqueville's thesis. In his poem "Lenin Before God" the Muslim poet Iqbal notes how the Russian church's close association with the czar made the religious leaders vulnerable to attack at the time of the revolution.[7]

The effort by democratic societies to get away from imposing control by force and to govern by consent is not a reversion to any previous model, but the development of a new and complex form of social and political life. Ideas from Greek experiments in the fifth century BCE and from the early Roman republic helped to legitimate the ideals of secularism, but essentially the Americans and others have been involved in creating new forms of social organization. The forms are new precisely because the process of governing is open to criticism by the citizens. It is essential for this, de Tocqueville said, that most citizens of these societies are literate and are informed by a free press.

The ideal of the consent of the governed is understood by most Christians as a valid way to implement the Christian ideal of the moral responsibility of free persons responsibly to exercise their individual judgments. We all know that mistakes are made much of the time, but the existence of errors of judgment does not change our commitment to the notion of responsibility. A young person coming to vote for the first time knows that he or she is entering into a covenant of responsibility for the well-being of the society as a whole.

If most people agree that it would not be advisable to change religious life and practice as often as we change political leaders, does this mean that religious institutions play no role in shaping the moral character of the citizens or influencing social and economic institutions? A key idea here is the notion of a voluntary association: citizens who feel strongly about a certain issue can join together to lobby the government and use the force of their common will to change laws and institutions. Voluntary associations such as the YMCA, the Boy Scouts and Girl Guides have become large autonomous institutions which serve a specific social purpose but are not linked directly to the government. The idea is that citizens should learn to look after many of their common problems without involving the government directly. Christian persons who feel strongly that certain changes must be made in society can try to implement such changes through non-governmental institutions, or they can try to put pressure on elected officials. Any Christian individual may run for public office. Canada's national health care system came largely as the result of the efforts of an elected official who had left his job as a Christian minister to run for parliament. There are many other instances of the successful implementation of reform by such persons.

Built into most contemporary European and North American societies is the idea of continual adaptation and change as the people decide what new forms of social institutions to develop. The abolition of slavery and the granting of voting rights to women are two new developments not envisaged by the earlier founders; and the design of the society permits this possibility. Most Christians understand themselves as fellow citizens with other persons in this type of secular society, and they recognize their obligations to protest and to order. What form protesting and ordering take will vary with the context.

Secularism means that changes must result from the consent of the people, not from the imposition of authoritarian rule legitimated by force. One of its primary affirmations is that military power should not be used to enforce conformity on the citizens. This restriction of the use of force is one of the main positive outcomes of the reforms instigated in many societies after the French and American revolutions.

The separation of church and state in the North American and European models means that the state does not interfere with the ongoing religious life of Christian people. The nurturing of Christian understanding and the shaping of Christian conscience takes place within the church. The individuals thus shaped must then enter into the wider society to exercise their judgment and wisdom as citizens. The scope available to the exercise of conscience is vast; it can involve speaking, writing and trying to influence opinion, many forms of public service, even founding new institutions. Christians can work through non-governmental or governmental institutions to try to bring about whatever reforms they consider necessary; and in the last two hundred years much positive reform has come about, in the development of hospitals for instance, but much remains to be done. New problems also continue to arise, such as the threat to the atmosphere by pollution. Therefore a kind of moral alertness, well-informed by a free press and media is necessary, as de Tocqueville predicted.

A further reason for the acceptance of secularism following de Tocqueville's model is a new commitment to human equality. De Tocqueville said the members of the French aristocracy, of whom he was one, conceived of themselves as the only "real" human beings and had not generally considered human beings of other social classes, especially the poor, as authentic human beings for whom they had any kind of responsibility.[8] He discovered something new within the social order in America: equality of citizenship was taken seriously and mutual responsibility was genuine. This meant, he again emphasized, the importance of newspapers and continuing communication among citizens so the people could be encouraged to understand each other's problems and difficulties and to accept mutual responsibility. While this would not be easy, de Tocqueville recognized that force was the only alternative. He saw the problem as an ongoing one of educating the imagination so that people of the future, unlike the French aristocrats of his acquaintance, could learn to imagine and to sympathize with the real experiences and lives of other persons.

One who has lived through a brutal revolution and the collapse of a social order as de Tocqueville did, especially a process as arbitrary and cruel as that of the French revolution, is not likely to survive it without developing considerable appreciation of the destructive capacities of human beings. This French aristocrat was not naive about how human beings could torment and destroy each other. He saw hope in the new experiment of democracy, but he did not imagine it would be without problems. He did hope, though, that the days of arbitrary tyranny supported by military power were finished and that the new structures of liberty, equality and fraternity would open new possibilities for people to be more effective in protesting injustice and working to order the common structures of life in a more just manner.

* * *

To keep both the "protesting" and the "ordering" images active in consciousness involves a continual readiness to protest specific aspects of any status quo in order to move forward to a better ordering of common existence. But any new ordering creates structures that will in their turn also be subject to protest and reform. For this reason, most Christians consider that there is no perfect system to be found in the past, but that the imperative is to move forward in ongoing efforts to discover better ways of implementing justice and compassion.

NOTES

[1] Norman Daniel, *Islam and the West*, Edinburgh, University Press, repr. 1962.

[2] For a discussion of the conversion of Constantine see Robin Lane Fox, *Pagans and Christians*, New York, Knopf, 1989.

[3] For a discussion of the early history of the Muslim community see M.A. Shaban, *Islamic History: A New Interpretation*, 2 vols, Cambridge, Cambridge UP, 1976.

[4] Fazlur Rahman, *Islamic Methodology in History*, Karachi, Central Institute of Islamic Research, 1965, pp.1-84.

[5] Niyazi Berkes, *The Rise of Secularism in Turkey*, Montreal, McGill UP, 1960.

[6] Alexis de Tocqueville, *Democracy in America*, tr. George Lawrence, New York, Doubleday, 1969, pp.295ff.

[7] V.G. Kiernan, tr. *Poems from Iqbal*, London, John Murray, 1955, p.42.

[8] *Op. cit.*, pp.562ff.

2. *Sharī'ah* and Modernity

WALID SAIF

The title "*Sharī'ah* and Modernity" implicitly suggests a conflict which calls for reconciliation. Even if this suggested conflict may turn out to have no theoretical basis, the present situation in the Muslim world in general shows that the relationship between the two is problematic, a source of much debate and dispute, complicated by a prevailing atmosphere of uncertainty, confusion, ambiguity and misconceptions.

The point of view adopted here is that conflict between *Sharī'ah* and modernity is neither necessary nor inherent.

Considering the relationship between *Sharī'ah* and modernity requires examining the meanings and implications of each.

The meaning of *Sharī'ah*

In Arabic *Sharī'ah* originally means "the path" or "the way". Within the Islamic religious framework it refers to the way of life to which Muslims should commit themselves: the prescribed set of rules, laws, values, criteria, behavioural patterns and worship practices which are supposed to organize and guide Muslim life both individually and collectively. Part of *Sharī'ah* in this sense is the responsibility of the individual, the other part is the responsibility of the collective institution or the state.

Nevertheless, the rules and values of *Sharī'ah* are meant to fulfil what are called in Arabic *maqāṣid al-sharī'ah*, meaning the aims, purposes and goals of *Sharī'ah*, which represent the frame of reference or the criteria for evaluating the practical results of the implementation of *Sharī'ah* and *fiqh* (Islamic jurisprudence). If those purposes are not fulfilled, it follows that the actual practices and applications are not in compliance with the spirit of *Sharī'ah* and its aims. *Maqāṣid al-sharī'ah* comprise social justice, equality and everything considered to be in the interest and for the welfare of both the individual and the community.

Obviously, although the general principles and purposes of *Sharīʻah* are constant, the practical definition of interests and welfare depends on circumstances, context and situation and is therefore changeable. This was expressed clearly by many great Muslim *fuqahā'* (*Sharīʻah* jurists) in both theoretical and practical terms. An important directive in *Sharīʻah* states that contrived *Sharīʻah* laws may be changed as a result of changes in time and places. For example, Al-Shāfiʻī, the founder of a famous school of Islamic jurisprudence, gave two different juridical answers to the same question directed to him in Iraq and Egypt, justifying this by the differences in the circumstances between the two places. The constant in each case was the purpose of *Sharīʻah*, that is, the welfare of people in view of the conditions of their situation.

What are called in *Sharīʻah* terminology *al maṣāliḥ al mursalah* (the open common interests) constitute a major source for Muslim *fuqahā'* to draw on in producing rules and laws to meet new needs. Obviously the definition of such standing interests requires collective institutionalized activity involving both *fuqahā'* and specialists in politics, economics, society and other fields. If the application of a certain pre-defined rule proves to contradict what are considered to be the current interests of the society and its individuals, then that rule may be suspended as long as that situation prevails. On the other hand, new directives and laws may be produced based on the general *Sharīʻah* principles to meet the emerging practical needs in the here and now.

Linked to this is the *Sharīʻah* principle that "necessities permit what otherwise is prohibited" — *al ḍarūrāt tubīh al-maḥẓūrāt*. For example, a Muslim may eat and drink what is otherwise prohibited by *Sharīʻah* in circumstances where that is necessary for the maintenance of his life and the protection of his well-being. A related *Sharīʻah* principle states that "no practice should cause damage to self or others" — *lā ḍarūrah wa lā ḍarār* — meaning that any undertaking, including religious practice, that would result in damage or harm to self or others should be avoided as contrary to the purposes of *Sharīʻah* in those specific situations. This general *Sharīʻah* principle is complemented by another one which rules that "avoiding damage and harm overrides acquiring benefits" — *dar'u al-mafāsid khayrun min jalb al-manāfiʻ* — meaning that if the conceivable results of a certain activity, including religious activity, include damage and mischief that would outweigh intended benefits, that activity should then be stopped or suspended.

In general, the application of a *Sharī'ah* rule or directive must be viewed within the overall *Sharī'ah* system and not in isolation, ensuring that citizens' rights and privileges are fulfilled and secured before requiring them to pay their dues and carry out their obligations, therefore judging them accordingly.

Unfortunately, many people — both Muslims and non-Muslims — tend to reduce *Sharī'ah* and its system of jurisprudence (*fiqh*) to its sub-system of punishment laws, which seem very strict, even harsh. Thus the idea of an Islamic state is associated exclusively with such punishment laws. This oversimplification ignores the fact that the punishment system constitutes only a small and limited element of the overall *Sharī'ah* system. In addition to the fact that the punishment laws can be applied only after a Muslim state has realized its defined obligations towards society of ensuring social justice, equality and civil rights, the circumstances in which they may be applied in practice are limited, involving a complex of conditions and proofs beyond the slightest doubt or suspicion. A general *Sharī'ah* rule states that "pre-defined punishments are precluded by doubts and suspicions" — *tudra' al ḥudūd bil shubuhāt*. In view of the accumulated *fiqh* material, the concept of *shubhah* — doubt and suspicion — is not confined to the nature of the available evidence, but also includes circumstances surrounding the event and the accused which may be interpreted as punishment-reducing factors, such as the material, mental and psychological state of the accused at the time of the crime. The second Rāshidi caliph, 'Umar Ibn al Khaṭṭāb, suspended the application of the theft punishment during a time of famine and general economic crisis, when the state failed to provide for the needy. Of course, this did not amount to approving theft or allowing it to prevail without state interference, but the pre-defined harsh punishment for theft was replaced by milder punishment during the crisis. The underlying assumption was that the general pre-conditions for the application of the punishment law were lacking.

Moreover, if we look in depth and with insight into the principles and aims of *Sharī'ah* together with the recorded practices of the Prophet and his companions, we can deduce that in cases of individual sins punishable by Islamic law *Sharī'ah* prefers sincere repentance by the sinner and preaching, persuasion and guidance by other individuals to producing incriminating evidence and applying punishment. Individual sinners are thus encouraged to repent and give up unlawful practices in the context of their individual private relationship with God instead of coming forward on their free own will to the legal institution for confession and therefore punishment. For sincere repentance is believed to erase sins and free sinners in the eyes of God without official institutional punishment.

On the other hand, individuals who witness others' sins are encouraged not to report the incidents with the necessary proof but privately to give guidance to the sinners. This *Sharī'ah* directive applies especially to individual sins which do not threaten the general social order. An example of this took place during the life of the Prophet. A man came to the Prophet and confessed adultery, asking to be punished according to Islamic law so that he would be freed from his sin. It is recorded that the Prophet gave him every chance to go back on his confession, but the man insisted. Later, a friend of that man disclosed to the Prophet that it was he who had persuaded him to confess and to turn himself over for punishment. The Prophet was displeased, saying that it would have been better had he just educated his friend and saved him exposure and punishment.

These remarks on the spirit, principles and purposes of *Sharī'ah* show that it comprises both constants and variables. Thus it should not be viewed as a static and rigid system of pre-defined and fixed laws and answers applicable to all conceivable cases in all times and places. Yet, many people — both proponents and opponents — mistakenly construe *Sharī'ah* and its system of *fiqh* as a completed body of knowledge which is assigned absolute truth value, rendering it an ahistorical entity engulfing time and space instead of interacting with them through human activity. A more realistic and rational view allocates a large part of the accumulated *fiqh* material to its historical and social context. Certainly, some basic principles and laws can be described as constants and strictly pre-defined. These are principles and laws stated in the Qur'ān and in well-documented Sunnah in a direct exclusive language which does not admit of different interpretations. But these constitute only a limited part of the accumulated *fiqh*. At the same time, even a good part of the Quranic text allows varied interpretations, and these are actually reflected in the works of Muslim jurists.

Furthermore, Qur'ān and Sunnah are not the exclusive sources of *Sharī'ah* and *fiqh*, although they represent a general framework for other sources. Another major source is *ijtihād*, which is essentially a human intellectual activity practised by competent Muslim jurists in the light of their understanding of the general principles and purposes of *Sharī'ah* and their assessment of contextual interests and necessities. Therefore, the results of *ijtihād* cannot be assigned absolute truth value surpassing changes of time and place. New circumstances produce new questions and needs which require new *Sharī'ah* directives through the continuous process of *ijtihād*. As a situated human activity, the process of *ijtihād* has always been influenced by the current socio-cultural atmosphere. Thus, its results should always be viewed and measured against their general social and historical background, and the sacredness of the divine revelation in the form of the holy Qur'ān should not be projected on the opinions of Muslim jurists.

Some people think that reviving institutional *Sharī'ah* in a Muslim state means reproducing past historical models. I believe, and many Muslim intellectuals share this view, that this is a major misconception. The common statement which has become almost a slogan: "Islam is suitable for all times and places" — *Al Islām ṣaliḥ li kulli zamān wa makān* — does not and should not imply that it is valid to reproduce past historical models of state and establishment, but rather that Islam offers a general framework which can be used to generate new models for new circumstances. In other words, the general principles of Islam and *Sharī'ah* may be projected against changing social backgrounds, thus producing new practical models which would meet emerging necessities and objective conditions and would offer answers to new questions. Such new models and answers are therefore the product of creative interaction between human interpretative activity, the Islamic frame of reference and social conditions. The results, irrespective of their forms, should always reflect the ultimate purposes of *Sharī'ah* which include social justice, equality, progress and happiness of the people.

The sources of *Sharī'ah*, including Qur'ān and Sunnah, are not texts of science or economics. Although they offer directives in these realms, they do not offer strict or alternative explanations for the forces of nature or laws of physics. Instead, they encourage people to explore nature, to look with insight within and outside the self, to discover the underlying laws and rules of natural and physical phenomena, to produce knowledge and to use it for the benefit of humankind. Islam lays down the moral values, guidelines and purposes of scientific knowledge that should direct and govern the human pursuit of knowledge to ensure that such undertaking is geared to serve human welfare. The relationship between humanity and nature is depicted in Islam as one of harmony and complementarity rather than one of conflict and domination.

Thus *Sharī'ah* is neither in opposition to nor in competition with science. Rather, religious and scientific systems are parallel and complementary, each representing a different level of reality. Adhering to one does not imply rejecting the other. In fact, Islam encourages scientific activity as a form of worship and as a tool for reinforcing religious belief.

The underlying assumption is that creations are concrete evidence of the absolute capability of the Creator. Scientific knowledge would lead to seeing the unity that underlies the diversity.

The meaning of modernity

Now we can turn to the question of the concept and meaning of modernity, which has also stirred much debate and dispute, resulting in many misconceptions. For many secular intellectuals in the Muslim world, Western civilization, manifested in the modern Western industrial secular state, is the universal model of modernity. Western civilization and culture are assigned absolute truth value and universal viability and validity.

One underlying assumption of this conception is that modern Western culture is the product of a scientific, rational and objective mode of thought. As such, its field of cognitive activity is objective reality; its tools and methods are experimental, empirical and rational. Consequently, its resultant body of knowledge is objective and value-free, and it is thus assigned an absolute truth-value which makes it applicable in any other socio-cultural context and qualifies it as a universal frame of reference for measuring and judging other cultures. Western civilization is therefore the universal model of progress and development.

Related to this is the assumption that the Western historical pattern of socio-economic change and development towards industrialization represents a universal pattern which all societies have to undergo in the course of progress. Yet, the West has gone so far in this kind of progress, thus constantly widening the gap between developed and developing countries, that the latter have no choice but to short-circuit normal developmental stages and affiliate with the Western imperial centre, importing ready-made knowledge, technology and developmental models.

A third assumption is that Western-style secularization is an inevitable condition of modernization and development. It is assumed that only when Europe had replaced the theocratic state by the secular one were the conditions for modernization created. Democracy and civil equality as pre-conditions for modernity are usually attributed exclusively to the secular state. By way of analogy, it is argued that only by relinquishing institutional *Sharīʻah* may Muslim societies achieve modernity.

This line of thought has always met with strong opposition in the Muslim world, accused of preaching alienation and Westernization and fostering colonial domination. As an extreme reaction, the Muslim world has been witnessing movements that preach cultural isolation for the sake of protecting national cultural identity.

The resulting conflict has for some time seemed irreconcilable, presenting only a choice between two types of alienation: either alienation into the historical past of the collective self or alienation into the present of the other, namely the West. Although contradictory in appearance, both represent negative and passive responses to the challenge of the dominant Western culture.

But a new and different mode of thinking, which transcends the above dichotomy, is now emerging in the Arab and Muslim world and gaining growing credibility. According to this line of thought, which draws on modern sociological and anthropological knowledge, modernity should not be defined exclusively in terms of the Western model, which must be placed in its own historical and socio-cultural context peculiar to the West itself.

In general, modernity means development, progress and positive change at all levels of social life and human activity. Yet, although interaction with world cultures and experiences is both inevitable and necessary, modernity should emerge from the objective conditions and within the historical context of a particular society, drawing on its own material, spiritual and cultural resources. The failure of developmental plans in developing countries is often due, at least in part, to having imported models that do not relate strongly enough to the local socio-economic and socio-cultural context, so that the society cannot interact with them in a positively productive way.

Furthermore, modernization must be a comprehensive process striking a balance of material, moral, spiritual, social, educational and cultural aspects. Many developmental plans in developing countries seem to fail partly because they are not sensitive to national culture and concentrate on consumer-oriented material development, ignoring the equal need for cultural development and thus causing social confusion, tension and conflict of value systems and cultural resources. In such a situation extremist movements of isolationism are likely to emerge and be reinforced. Thus, in view of the fact that Islam and *Sharī'ah* values are deeply rooted in the Muslim collective conscience and form a major foundation of Muslim culture, any process of modernization and development that proves insensitive to these will certainly be met with resentment and failure.

Several other misconceptions about modernity are now being seen in a new light. For example, the Western secular state should be seen as having replaced not Christianity as a faith and culture, but the theocratic political institution which was an historical reality but not an inherent component of the Christian faith. Christianity, therefore, has continued to be a basic foundation of Western culture and civilization at all levels of institutional life. Yet, the analogy between the historic Islamic state and the European theocratic state is not accurate. By definition an Islamic state is not and has never been a theocratic state governed by clergy or by a ruler who derives authority from an assumed absolute divine mandate. A Muslim ruler in an Islamic state is required to observe *Sharī'ah* principles, but he cannot, in principle, assume the authority to define it or be a source of *Sharī'ah* and *fiqh*. The sharp contrast between secularism and the theocratic state as known in the West in past times does not apply in the Islamic context, since an Islamic state is not a theocratic one in the first place. It may then be said that while the Western secular state is not equivalent to a non-Christian state, the Islamic state on the other hand is not, in theory, equivalent to a theocratic state.

The concept of a secular state is usually proclaimed as a prerequisite for securing civil equality among all citizens irrespective of their faiths. In fact, *Sharī'ah* assumes such required equality unconditionally. The Prophet states clearly that "all people are equal like the teeth of the comb" — *al nās sawāsiyatun ka asnān al-mishṭ*. The equal right of all to practise their faith without interference is ensured by the holy Qur'ān. A Quranic verse states that "there should be no coercion in religion". Yet has the secular state really ensured equality? Certainly the concept of equality is not confined to religious freedom. What about the vast class differences which the modern secular capitalist state has created within its own society? What about the long history of ethnic and religious conflicts which have been experienced in the modern secular state and which still persist? What about colonial domination, which has long subdued other nations? What about the greedy exhaustion of natural resources at the expense of future generations? Those are the types of inequality which have been practised by the very secular state which derived part of its legitimacy from its promise to ensure equality.

* * *

Global awareness is growing that modernity in its material manifestation should be more guided and balanced by moral values derived from religion in general, to ensure that it works for the real benefit of all humankind. Religion offers a holistic perspective in which one can perceive one's central position within the overall natural system whose elements are interdependent and interactive. This may be seen as a common ground where Islam, Christianity and other world religions may meet, interact and cooperate. Islam recognizes the harmonious unity of humanity and nature, and while it encourages scientific knowledge and material progress it lays down for them guidelines, directives and principles which are not different from those of *Sharī'ah*.

In view of the above remarks and observations, it can be concluded that *Sharī'ah* does not hinder but rather encourages modernity in its broader sense. *Sharī'ah* can, in fact, be a powerful drive for development, progress and scientific discovery, but is surely concerned with the ultimate ends and purposes of these. Finally, it lies in the hands of the people themselves to interpret *Sharī'ah* values and concepts in such a positive, practical and productive way as to achieve its purposes in the interest of all.

3. The Implications of *Sharī'ah*, *Fiqh* and *Qānūn* in an Islamic State

TAYYIB Z. AL-ABDIN

Definition of terms

The word *Sharī'ah* occurs in the Qur'ān referring to the way of God as he revealed it to his prophets; "Then we put thee on the right way (*Sharī'ah*) of religion: so follow thou that way, and follow not the desires of those who know not" (45:18).

This is not confined to the religion of Islam, but is the totality of God's commandments as conveyed by a prophet to a particular society.[1] Muslims believe that the commandments which are binding for them are only those included in the Qur'ān and the authentic traditions of the Prophet. In Islam those commandments encompass all aspects of life: creed (*'aqīdah*), forms of worship (*'ibādāt*), transactions (*mu'āmalāt*), principles of government, prescribed punishments (*ḥudūd*), family law and moral rules (*akhlāq*). Believers are obliged to follow all these commandments to the best of their ability, with the sincere intention of following God's way. The believer who is following these commandments is in a state of worship for which he shall be rewarded by God in this life and in the hereafter. Some of these commandments are of a collective nature and cannot be implemented by an individual person. Hence, the responsibility of realizing such commandments becomes a collective one. The individual's role is to demonstrate a readiness to share in these activities. Other commandments can be carried out only by the rulers in society. The society is responsible to choose rulers who are willing to fulfil these commandments and to urge their fulfilment upon whoever rules. The basic characteristic of the Islamic resurgence during the last three decades is the call for the implementation of *Sharī'ah* in public affairs as well as in personal life.[2]

The word *fiqh* is used in the Qur'ān in the verb form meaning "to know" or "to comprehend". As a technical term it means jurisprudence, the science of religious law in Islam. As *Sharī'ah* is a comprehensive way of life, so is *fiqh*. It covers all aspects of religious, political and civil life. *Fiqh* is the human science by which we know or interpret the commandments of God as revealed to us in the *Sharī'ah*,[3] the Qur'ān and the Sunnah. *Fiqh* is the science of giving a specific ruling on a particular case by studying the relevant text in Qur'ān and Sunnah and investigating the circumstances of the case. The room for human discretion is very wide in *fiqh*, especially in those areas which are subject to change according to time and place, such as transactions, public affairs, principles of government and the like. That is why Islam has institutionalized *ijtihād* (human judgment) as the third source of *Sharī'ah* after Qur'ān and Sunnah. The more widely *ijtihād* is accepted, the better it is. If acceptance reaches a consensus (*ijmā'*), *ijtihād* becomes perfect. It is unlikely to find a religion which encourages *ijtihād* as much as Islam does. Even a wrong *ijtihād* is rewarded by God once, while a correct one is doubly rewarded.[4]

Whenever the authencity of the text is not absolutely certain (not all Sunnah is authentic) or its meaning not absolutely clear, there is room for a new interpretation and a new *ijtihād*. *Ijtihād* is specifically called for:

1) if a new situation arises for which there is no reference in Qur'ān or Sunnah;
2) when a text is inconsistent with the general objectives of *Sharī'ah* – the preservation of religion, life, offspring, intellect and property;
3) if the text is general or vague;
4) in a case where two different texts may be applied.

In these cases the *faqīh* or scholar is duty-bound to give an *ijtihād* that suits the particular circumstances and observes the general principles of the *Sharī'ah*.

The wide range for human judgment in *fiqh* meant that various schools of *fiqh* (*Madhāhib*) flourished in the history of Islam, of which the major ones are Ḥanafī, Malikī, Ḥanbalī, Shāfi'ī and Ja'farī (a Shi'ī *Madhhab*). None was associated with the government of the time; indeed, most of them spread among common Muslims despite the opposition of the government of the day. As there is no formal class of clergy in Islam, anyone well versed in Islamic sciences is eligible to make his own ruling on a specific problem. However, the populace usually goes for the ruling of a scholar whom they trust for his piety and knowledge. Like other religions, Islam has known both conservative and liberal interpretations of the text: certain schools of *fiqh* (the Salafiyyah) are known for their literal reading of the text while others (the school of *ra'y* or opinion) go by the wisdom behind the text.

The word *qānūn*, which means "law", is not originally an Arabic word but of Greek origin. It crept into Muslim vocabulary in the fifteenth century when the Ottoman sultans started to borrow some portions of European laws, mainly in the area of administration and finance. Later it spread through the imposition of European secular laws by Western colonial powers. In Muslim religious circles *qānūn* denotes codes and regulations derived partly or wholly from Western laws. Some Islamic universities have a "faculty of *Sharī'ah* and *qānūn* law", in order to signify the distinction between the two. Countries which proclaim *Sharī'ah* as their only source of legislation avoid using *qānūn* for laws borrowed from Western sources; Saudi Arabia, for example, uses the word *naẓām* instead. At the same time, they call the agencies which judge according to these laws "committees" rather than "courts". However, most Muslim countries today use the word *qānūn* for the enacted laws, whether or not they are based on *Sharī'ah* principles: the Syrian Code (*qānūn*) of Personal Status (1953), the Iraqi Code (*qānūn*) of Personal Status (1959), the Egyptian Family Code (1960) and the recent Sudanese Criminal Code (1991). All these laws are based on the *Sharī'ah* but adopt the term *qānūn*. Nevertheless, for the purpose of this paper it is useful to maintain the distinction between the two terms made in Muslim religious circles: that *qānūn* is a law not derived from the *Sharī'ah*.

Implications in an Islamic state

What are the implications of these terms in an Islamic state? The shortest definition of an Islamic state is to say that it is the government of *Sharī'ah*. The major characteristic of the Islamic state is that it rules according to the injunctions of *Sharī'ah*.

Although *Sharī'ah* is the supreme law, which no authority has the power to repeal, the Islamic state is a popular government in the sense that it represents the convictions of the people and its rulers must be installed by the will of the people. The limitation on the rulers' authority is a guarantee of the prevalence of the religious will of the community. Nevertheless, there remains a wide area for legislation and *ijtihād*, as explained earlier. As there is no formal class of clergy in Islam, the Islamic state should not degenerate into a theocratic government. Even the Shi'ah denomination, which recognizes a hierarchical class of *'ulamā'*, made the selection of its rulers an open electoral contest in the Islamic Republic of Iran. The same is expected to happen in Afghanistan and Sudan. It is interesting to note that almost all the leaders of the contemporary Islamic resurgence in the Muslim world do not belong to the *'ulamā'* class: Muḥammad Ḥāmid Abu al-Nasr of Egypt (farmer), 'Abbasi Madanī of Algeria (professor of education), Ḥassan al-Turābī of Sudan (professor of constitutional law), Rāshid al-Ghanoushī of Tunisia (teacher of philosophy), Qazi Hussain Ahmad of Pakistan (teacher of geography), Gulbuddin Hekmatyar of Afghanistan (engineer), Najm al-Din Arbakan of Turkey (professor of engineering). The *'ulamā'* class tend to support the status quo and not opt for a radical change. However, it is difficult for them to argue against the demands of the Islamic resurgence which call for the rule of *Sharī'ah*.

Establishing a state which fulfils the commandments of God is a central idea in Islam. It was the Prophet Muḥammad who founded the first government in central Arabia. He was the Prophet and the statesman of that first Muslim society. The Muslims felt the need to choose a successor before they buried the body of their Prophet. His immediate successors were those who served best the cause of Islam, worked closely with the Prophet and were known for their piety and knowledge of religion. Thereafter the history of the Muslim world was inseparably linked with the history of the caliphate until its abolition in Istanbul 1924. The caliphate was the only institution responsible for the custody of the faith and the protection of the believers. The activists who work for an Islamic state not only hope to achieve the rule of *Sharī'ah* in their respective countries but also aspire to ignite a renaissance in the Muslim world, reviving the old glory of Islam. Looking for a strong and united Muslim *Ummah* and a just and moral society, they abhor the decadence and weakness of the present Muslim world. This is why the majority of the Islamists are likely to adopt a liberal interpretation of *Sharī'ah* in order to achieve its objectives rather than its literal dictates. However, the word "liberal" here should not be read in a Western context.

Although the heritage of *fiqh* which the Muslims have accumulated over the centuries is second to none in the history of jurisprudence, covering all aspects of human activity, Islamists realize that it is not good enough to meet all the requirements of a modern society and a modern state. In the important areas of government institutions and functions, the *Sharī'ah* has set some basic principles but not detailed systems. It is up to Muslims at different times and different places to work out the detailed systems which suit them within the bounds of those basic principles. For example, the Qur'ān and the traditions of the Prophet instruct the

Muslims to make decisions in public affairs through *al-shūrā* or consultation (Qur'ān 42:38; 3:159).

The best guided caliphs (*al-khulafa' al-Rāshidūn*) who succeeded the Prophet implemented this principle of *al-shūrā* in different ways. The Prophet died without specifying to his companions how to choose a successor. Different ways were practised within a short period of 30 years, but all agreed that the new caliph should have the free consent of the believers. A similar behaviour was adopted in the areas of administration, economy and education. The Muslim scholars should develop their *fiqh* in these areas in order to fulfil the objectives of *Sharī'ah*. The principles and the objectives are fixed, but the forms and systems differ from time to time.

Fiqh is based not only on the texts in the Qur'ān and the Sunnah but also on the practical conditions to which these texts are to be applied. The interaction between the text and the situation shows the validity or invalidity of the ruling. During the degeneration of Muslim thought, the traditional *'ulamā'* closed the door of *ijtihād*, fearing that any innovation would only harm the excellence of *fiqh* as perfected by the forefathers. For centuries, the Muslims lived on the *fiqh* heritage of those forefathers. Some enlightened Ottoman sultans felt the need for new *ijtihād* in certain areas but could not find the competent *'ulamā'* to help them. The late sultans turned towards Europe to borrow certain laws and institutions. During the centuries when the *fiqh* did not interact with practical problems of life and withdrew to the background, it left the stage for secular Western thought to dominate. The impact of 19th- and 20th-century Western civilization on the Muslim world was shattering. It showed clearly how seriously Muslim thought was lagging behind, and this convinced many educated Muslims and leaders to follow blindly the European path of civilization. The gap today is too big between the state of *fiqh* and the requirements of present-day life. This is why some Muslim leaders, like Dr Turābī of Sudan, have argued that the development of *fiqh* has to be planned and institutionalized in order to fill that gap.[5] In other words, Muslims should not depend only on individual voluntary efforts to develop *fiqh* in order to meet the requirements of the time.

Who are the competent *'ulamā'* to make *ijtihād* for present-day problems? Traditional religious education, which is concerned with the study of Qur'ān, Sunnah and the classic *fiqh* books, does not qualify the scholar to know the practical problems of the world. The tendency in recent years has been for the idea of a grand mufti to give way to councils of *iftā'* which include religious scholars as well as experts in various fields. Such councils exist in Iran, Pakistan, Sudan and Saudi Arabia. All Islamic banks have a *Sharīʻah* committee, which includes religious scholars as well as economists and bankers and has the power to reject any transaction that does not conform with the Islamic principles. Moreover, a *fatwā* or *ijtihād* made in one society is not necessarily good for other societies. The particular conditions of each society influence the solutions which suit that society. In other words, there is no single Islamic solution for the same problem appearing at the same time in different societies.

Can an Islamic state borrow laws (*qawānīn*) and institutions from other cultures? The Salafī school of thought holds that any substantive legislation which allows or prohibits things should be derived from *Sharīʻah* sources alone. Along these lines, a 45-page memorandum, signed by more than a hundred young *'ulamā'* in Saudi Arabia, was presented to King Fahd in July 1992. It stated that deriving any legislation from the French penal code or from the Egyptian civil code is completely forbidden in Islam, no matter whether the legislation is in conformity with the *Sharīʻah* or not.[6] However, most contemporary scholars, including the leaders of Islamic movements, accept the principle that wisdom is the objective of the believer, and wherever it is found it may be taken. Dr Al-Turābī argues that "we may benefit from the experience of humanity and their customs in realizing justice and in adopting means to fulfil objectives".[7] Therefore, *qawānīn* from other cultures may be adopted in an Islamic state as long as they serve the general objectives of *Sharīʻah* and do not contradict any clear text. At the same time, it may not be desirable for an emerging Islamic state to rush into borrowing laws from different quarters to the extent of weakening its own distinct characteristics. When the early Muslims borrowed ideas and institutions from the Persians, Romans or Greeks, it did not endanger their cultural personality because it was done from a position of strength. The Muslims of today cannot make the same claim.

Sharīʻah and the Islamic state are often associated today with *ḥudūd*, the prescribed punishments. *Ḥudūd* cover only eight offenses, nearly all of which are also mentioned in the Old Testament and half of which are not applicable to non-Muslims. The punishments are severe but the evidence required to prove them is exceedingly strict. There can be no *ijtihād* on the punishments themselves, but there is a place for *ijtihād* in the area of procedure and evidence. However, the number of *ḥudūd* offenses does not merit the propaganda created around them.

In conclusion one may say that an Islamic state is a state based on the principles of *Sharī'ah*. The *Sharī'ah* itself is finite, but the forms of its application and the richness of its interpretation are infinite. After all, the spirit of *Sharī'ah* is more important than its letter and its objectives more valuable than the text.

The challenge facing Muslims is to develop their *fiqh* of the *Sharī'ah* in order to meet the demands of modernity and progress. The Western world, whose modern civilization began five hundred years ago through the encouragement of new ideas and values, should tolerate the emergence of cultures based on other ideas and values. The West itself has undergone a transformation of values and ideas through the passage of time. How could the West claim that it has said the last word about anything? The tremendous technological and material progress it has achieved does not hide some serious weaknesses in Western society, and the cure for some of these may be found in other cultures. Religiously minded people in any culture should be happy when people take religion seriously and seek to implement its values in all areas of life.

NOTES

1 M.A. Al-Tahnāwī, *Kashaf Istilāḥāt al Funūn*, (Beirut, Dar Sadir, n.d.), Vol.II; also Al Jurjānī, Kitāb al-Ta'rīfāt.

2 Cf. J.L. Esposito, *Voices of Resurgent Islam*, New York, Oxford UP, 1983.

3 Cf. Al-Tahanāwī, *op. cit.*

4 Ibn Mājah, 2335, Al Aẓamī (ed.)

5 Ḥassan al Turābī, *Manhajiyyat al Fiqh wa al-Tashri'al-Islāmī*, Khartoum, 1987, p.11.

6 "Mudhakirāt al-Nasīḥa", in *Al-Jazīrah al-'Arabiyyah*, Oct. 1992.

7 *Op. cit.*

Part II

4. *Sharī'ah*, Change and Plural Societies

JØRGEN S. NIELSEN

Law in theory, content, and practice

The three concepts of *Sharī'ah*, *fiqh* and *qānūn* form a useful starting point in considering Muslim responses to the modern world, in terms of both aiding an analysis of the substrata often hidden in the emotional use of the term *Sharī'ah* and deconstructing some of the historical myths that surround it.

Both classically and currently, Muslims have often used *Sharī'ah* and *fiqh* as synonyms. In a pre-modern situation, where Islamic civilization had accumulated centuries of experience in the field of Islamic law, this is hardly surprising. The distinction, part of the foundational theology, had with time become one of theory with little practical import. But that the distinction is there is betrayed by the recurring analysis of the science of Islamic jurisprudence into its "roots" (*uṣūl al-dīn*) and "branches" (*furū' al-fiqh*), clearly implying that *fiqh* is the human science of deducing from basic principles and sources, using specific intellectual techniques, what the detailed provisions for human action should be, individually and collectively, so that women and men may reach fulfilment and blessing (*falāḥ*) in this world and the next.

Sharī'ah, then, is the theological foundation and structure which the *fiqh* interprets and fills in. It is thus no coincidence that the phrase used for discussing the divine purpose is the "intentions of the *Sharī'ah*" (*maqāṣid al-sharī'ah*), rather than the intentions of the *fiqh*, for the role of the *fiqh* is to seek the implementation of those intentions. There is no doubt that since mediaeval times both Muslim scholars and outside observers have tended to confuse the two — easily done given the usual lack of practical consequences.

With this distinction in mind, the idea of the "immutability" of the *Sharī'ah*, propounded in classical Islamic authorities, picked up by

Western commentators and echoed by modern Muslim thinkers, takes on a different connotation from what it often has today. It is the fundamental purposes and principles of the Islamic law (the *Sharī'ah*) which are God-given, not their detailed implementation (the *fiqh*). The latter is the product of particular contexts of time and place. It is therefore possible for the provisions of the law to change and develop as necessary and appropriate. This view was expressed and implemented by leading Muslim theologians and jurists throughout the mediaeval period in the face of a widespread timidity among the professional jurist-theologians (*'ulamā'*) to challenge the inherited teachings of the great masters of previous generations. The "closing of the gate of independent reasoning (*ijtihād*)" during the mediaeval period was never generally accepted.

The concept of *qānūn* brings a different aspect of the Islamic law into the discussion, namely the relationship between government, the courts and the religious institution of the *'ulamā'*. *Qānūn* was used in the Ottoman period to denote that aspect of government-sponsored regulation and its implementation which lay outside the *fiqh* and its implementation, namely the court of the Islamic judge, the *qāḍī*. This was not felt to be foreign to the legitimate practice of an Islamic government. Although the term was new, deriving from Greek, the practice was a continuation of the field of governmental discretion to which previous regimes and dynasties had given other names — *siyāsah* and *maẓālim*, to mention two of the better known.

As *qānūn* is the term most frequently used in Arabic today to describe legislation and codes of law, it is important to place it historically. First, before the modern period, opposition to *qānūn* came from the theologian-jurists primarily for institutional reasons: it was considered a competitor to the *fiqh*-based institutions. The legitimacy of the *qānūn* system was called into question only by the most zealous of Islamic ideologists. Second, the *qānūn* was not the primary route through which Western challenges to the Ottoman system infiltrated. Rather, the special privileges granted — originally, as early as the 16th century, from a position of power — by the Istanbul government to foreign traders and their communities under the so-called capitulations became the tool of European governments' interference and subversion of Ottoman sovereignty during the 19th century when the balance of power had changed.

This preliminary discussion suggests that a consideration of the response of *Sharī'ah* to the modern world has to take place around two interrelated sets of processes: on the one hand, a theological-juridical discussion of the relationship between Islamic principles (*Sharīʻah*) and their implementation (*fiqh*); on the other, the question of the relationships among *Sharīʻah*, religio-juridical institutions and state. The first is a conceptual discussion of fundamental significance for Muslim self-understanding and for outsiders' perceptions of Islam; the second is a socio-political question of immediate and long-term consequence for Muslim communities seeking to find ways of living in a mobile and plural world, not to mention for the communities who live alongside them.

Islamic law in change and development

As has been implied above, there is a strongly evolutionary element to *Sharīʻah*. In particular areas of the Islamic law, major debate and change have taken place as circumstances required. As examples one could mention the flexibility shown in the advice of some North African jurists to their fellow Muslims, left behind in Spain as Muslim governments gave way to the *reconquista* five centuries ago, or the gradual changes in Islamic land and rent law in the Ottoman empire during the 15th to 17th centuries, or the attitudes adopted by Muslim minority rulers over a Hindu majority in Moghul India.

The urgency of the challenge faced in the present century arises from the sheer pace of change, so accelerated that traditional processes of dialogue between theory and necessity have long since been left behind. It is this, rather than any essential characteristic, which occasionally may give the *Sharīʻah* the air of being regressive or conservative.

More significant is the fact that since the 18th century the energy for the accelerated change has come overwhelmingly from the West. This "West" may be conceived of in different ways — Christendom, the European powers, the industrial and post-industrial revolution, imperialism, secularism and the nation state, the US-led "free world", the "New World Order" — depending on the chronological and ideological starting point. But the essential fact remains that the locus for initiative, the setting of priorities, moved outside the Muslim world. Under such circumstances Muslims have sought to identify points in which to anchor their distinctiveness.

Thus it is that *Sharīʻah* has become one of the most potent symbols of the encounter — a modern *Kulturkampf* — between two civilizations which by any objective analysis have more in common than what divides them. On both sides, the demonization of the other tends to centre on *Sharīʻah*. In Western eyes, the Islamic state is one which implements barbaric punishments, persecutes non-Muslim minorities and suppresses women. In Muslim eyes, the West is atheistic, promiscuous, corrupt and — worst of all — anti-Islamic. Of course, there are elements of truth in both charges, but being based on a selective recording of events and a limited understanding of the complexities involved on both sides, they tempt participants in the encounter into confirming archaic prejudices. Consequently, both sides are easily seduced by media sensationalism and superficiality, misled by the special pleading of local factions seeking international support and rushed into reinforcing the unquestioned myths of their own positions. The common denominator of each side becomes fear of the other.

A number of views and experiences need to be fed into these relationships. Some are pointed to other papers in this volume, in particular the need for the Muslim world to break with the caricature of a monolithic secularistic civilization which has totally surrendered to materialistic "scientism" and relegated the spiritual life to a small private enclave. Here I will draw attention only to two elements in the 20th-century *Sharī'ah* experience of which outsiders must be aware if they are to make any judgment other than condemnation, thus contributing to self-fulfilling prophecies rather than opening the way to new modes of living together. Both elements are posited on my understanding of the basic flexibility and adaptability of the traditional *Sharī'ah*.

One effect of European domination over Muslim cultures has been the replacement (usually through redundancy rather than forced elimination) of traditional Islamic systems of education by systems modelled on European experiences. With few exceptions, the result has been a critical shortage of personnel with the learning and experience needed to implement *Sharī'ah* law in its full richness and flexibility when regimes have come to power with a populist appeal to the implementation of *Sharī'ah*. Certainly, most if not all of the incidents reported in the Western press as examples of the implementation of *Sharī'ah* provisions in many Muslim countries have been gross miscarriages of justice according to most traditional *Sharī'ah* conventions, carried out by people with only a slogan-like knowledge of traditional mainstream *fiqh*. One of the more encouraging aspects of the current Islamic revival would thus be the revival of a much more thorough training of large numbers of people in *Sharī'ah*.

A more optimistic indicator of the changes taking place — and of the possibility of fundamental changes apart from publicly articulated pressure — comes from some quite spectacular revolutions in traditional *Sharī'ah* positions. Some practical ones could be cited, such as the disappearance from the central encounter of any theoretical defence by Muslims of the traditional permission of slavery, in sharp contrast to the traditional permission of polygamy (more accurately polygyny) — both institutions being in a similar category of reluctantly permitted but limited and regulated by the Prophet.

Much more significant for some centrally inherited concepts of the relationship between *Sharīʿah* and the state, in both theology and institutions, is the increasingly active role some self-declaredly Islamic governments are taking in the formulation and codification of *Sharīʿah* law across a variety of fields. During the second and third centuries of Islamic history, the development of government institutions, ideas regarding the relationship between Islam and the state and the role of the religious professionals (the *ʿulamāʾ*) were sources of major political, social and cultural conflicts. Historically, the institutional foundations of Islamic law were decided to be outside the control of the state. The courts might be funded by government, but often were not, and the Islamic law they were called on to implement was outside the government's control. This was private religious lawyers' law, in which government interfered at its peril. The fact that this central classical principle has quietly fallen by the wayside in the last few decades is of enormous historical significance — and of still unpredictable consequences. Today, governments which call themselves Islamic are legislating and cooperating in attempts to codify Islamic law, whereas legislation and codification were traditionally anathema.

Among the most far-reaching consequences of these developments is the debate currently taking place among Muslim scholars, political leaders and governments in three fields:

— First is the process of defining *Sharīʿah,* in the knowledge that this is the divinely ordained order and therefore in principle immutable. The narrower and more theological in nature this definition is, the more scope there is for legal development; the wider and more legal the scope of this definition, the less room there is for the development of the law.

— Second, and closely related, is the room granted to the exercise of *ijtihād*. Very wide possibilities are already evident in areas such as economics and public administration. The debate is more acute in areas of the law which have seen some continuity of practice into the recent past and the present: criminal law, family law and the status of minorities. But potentially this can go deeper: to what extent may *ijtihād* be exercised with regard to the foundational principles of the law, the underlying theology or even the understanding of the Qur'ān? This is very sensitive territory.

- Third, what is the nature of the religio-political institution and its relationship to the state? Here the debate centres on a complex of issues of authority and location of control. Can the law be developed only by those learned in it — and learned according to particular scholarly traditions? May government institutions play a part? Or may the community as a whole also contribute, perhaps through methods made possible by modern technology, methods which could be regarded as being democratic, even if that term is rejected in some Islamic circles?

Part II

5. *Tashrī‘* (Process of Law-Making) in Islam

ASGHAR ALI ENGINEER

Sharī‘ah is the key to the practice of Islam, and it is considered as the manifestation of Islamic beliefs in practice. In order to be a true Muslim three things are needed: *iqrār bil-lisān* (acceptance of Islam with one's tongue), *iqrār bil-janān* (endorsement in one's heart) and *'amal bil-arkān* (practice through one's limbs). The third of these has to do with *Sharī‘ah*, the body of Islamic jurisprudence. *Sharī‘ah* is often mistakenly considered immutable by believing Muslims. As with other beliefs, the Muslims are divided into numerous *Madhāhib* (sects and schools of jurisprudence), and this division has persisted throughout Islamic history without being reconciled.

While *Sharī‘ah* has been an important source of legislation in most Islamic countries, laws based on *Sharī‘ah* have also raised many controversies, particularly in the areas of personal law (marriage, divorce, polygamy) and criminal punishment (chopping off hands of thieves, stoning adulterers to death). Many orthodox Muslims and the *'ulamā'* maintain that as these laws are divine they cannot be changed. Modernist Muslims, by contrast, feel that there is a need to rethink these issues, though within the Islamic framework. Debates and controversies continue between these two types of Muslims, and many non-Muslims have also expressed opinions on the matter.

What is the nature of these controversies? What is the process of evolution of *Sharī‘ah* in Islam? Are these laws really immutable or are they subject to change? What are the sources of legislation in Islam? Are all Muslims agreed on these sources or are there differences among them? Only by looking in detail at these vital questions can we understand the true significance of *tashrī‘* (law-making in Islam).

The important sources of legislation in Sunnī Islam are the Qur'ān, *Ḥadīth*, *qiyās* (analogy) and *ijmā‘* (consensus) and in Shi'ah Islam the

Qur'ān, *Ḥadīth* and the authority of the Imām. We should emphasize that what is known today as *Sharī'ah* did not come into existence during the Prophet's own lifetime. It took more than a century and the efforts of many a jurist for the Islamic legal corpus to evolve. The *Sharī'ah* in Shi'ah Islam began to be codified on the basis of what Imām Ja'far al Ṣādiq had pronounced on various matters pertaining to law; and Imām Ja'far lived 150 years after the *Hijrah* of the Prophet from Makkah to Al Madīnah.

The codification of *Sharī'ah* by different jurists after a lapse of more than a century following the death of the Prophet has an important bearing on the evolution of *Sharī'ah*. It is also important for our discussion that the concept of *Sharī'ah* itself evolved much later. It hardly existed in the first few centuries of Islamic history. Jurists in the earlier centuries use the term *Sharī'ah* only in passing if at all, or they used other forms from the root *sh-r-'*. In Imām Abū Ḥanifah's *al Fiqh al-Akbar* even the root *sh-r-'* does not occur. We do not find the concept of *Sharī'ah* as central even in Al Ash'arī's writings, particularly his *Maqālāt al-Islāmiyyīn*.

In the Qur'ān the word *Sharī'ah* occurs once (45:18): "Then We made thee follow a path in the matter [of religion], so follow it, and follow not the low desires of those who know not." Other different forms also occur, such as *shir'a, shur'an, al-shar'*. According to Imām Raghib, an authority on Quranic lexicography, *al-shar'* means "straight and clear path", and a clear path is also called *shar'un*, *shir'un* and *shari'atun*. The Qur'ān does not use the term *Sharī'ah* in its later sense of *corpus juris*. Nor do we find mention of the word in this sense except casually even in the writings of great Islamic thinkers, jurists and theologians like Al Ash'arī, Ibn Bābawayh, Al-Baqillānī, Al Baghdādī, Al Jūwaynī, Al Imām al Ghazālī, Al-Nasafī and Al-Shahrastānī. Thus the sense in which we use the word *Sharī'ah* today, as the body of Islamic laws, was not prevalent at least until the sixth century of Islam, after the classical or formative period.

It is necessary to examine all four principal sources of law-making and the controversies around them, since it is being maintained today that there were no controversies and that the entire body of Islamic laws developed without any human agency. In fact, in the entire process of formation of *Sharī'ah* human agency plays an important role. Though the Qur'ān is the principal source of Islamic *Sharī'ah*, as noted above, its understanding varies from person to person, including among the companions of the Prophet.

The Qur'ān and its understanding

There was no uniform understanding of the Quranic verses as they were revealed from time to time. The companions of the Prophet often differed from each other about their precise meanings. No wonder that commentaries on the Qur'ān written by eminent theologians and Islamic thinkers all differ from each other. Aḥmad Amīn, an eminent modern Egyptian Islamic scholar, notes in his classical work *Fajr al Islām* (Beirut, 1975) that the Qur'ān was revealed in the language, style and way of speaking of the Arabs. Its words were Arabic except for a few from other languages, which were Arabicized and became part of the Arabic language. This was quite natural: the Qur'ān came addressing the Arabs primarily. The Qur'ān says, "And we sent no messenger but with the language of his people, so that he might explain to them clearly" (14:4). Even so, the whole Qur'ān was not within the reach of all the companions of the Prophet. Nor does the fact that the Qur'ān was revealed in Arabic mean that all Arabs would understand every one of its individual and compound words. The understanding of any book depends not on language alone, but also on the degree to which one's intellect conforms with the intellectual level of the book. This also applies to the Arabs and the Qur'ān. Not all of them necessarily understood it fully, and they differed in their understanding of it.

Anas bin Malik reports that a person once asked 'Umar Ibn al Khaṭṭāb about the words of Allah' *wa fākihatan wa abban* ("and fruits and cattle feed"), what is *abban*? 'Umar replied that we are forbidden to go into depth and strain ourselves. Similarly, 'Umar once recited on the pulpit the Quranic verse which contains the word *takhawwuf* and enquired about its meaning. And we all know the status of 'Umar in matters of religion and knowledge. Then how about other companions?

In fact most of the companions were content with the overall sense of the verse and seldom bothered to go into the details of its meaning. Moreover, there are many verses in the Qur'ān for which it is not enough to know the meanings of their individual words. The Qur'ān itself says that there are verses which are decisive (*muḥkamāt*) and verses which are allegorical (*mutashabihāt*) (3:6). The former are concerned with the basis and principles of *Dīn* (religion), as in the Sūrat al-An'am, and these can be understood by common Arabs. The latter are difficult, and only a selected few can understand them.

Even though the companions of the Prophet were in general better qualified to understand the Qur'ān, as it was revealed in their language and they witnessed the circumstances in which it was revealed, they differed from each other over its understanding. Not all of them knew Arabic, but some knew more about the *Jāhiliyyah* (pre-Islamic literature) and hence were familiar with alien words, which helped them in understanding many Quranic words. Similarly, those who stayed by the side of the Prophet gained knowledge of the causes of revelation (*asbāb al-muzūl*) of the Quranic verses, which helped greatly in grasping the meaning of these verses, which could be quite misleading for those who did not. Those who knew more about Arab *'adāt* (customs) could better comprehend certain verses, for example, those pertaining to *Ḥajj*. Furthermore, those who knew about the practices of contemporary Christians and Jews in Arabia could understand certain verses better than those who did not. Knowledge of the meaning of Quranic verses also depended on one's knowledge of *Ḥadīth* literature, which, as we will see in the next section, is highly controversial.

From all this it is evident that on the understanding of the Qur'ān even the close companions of the Prophet differed from each other. Later this was also reflected in the formulation of the Islamic laws. Each jurist understood these verses in his own way and in the light of the *Ḥadīth* he relied upon. Thus although the source — the Qur'ān — is divine, its understanding is human and one's understanding of the Qur'ān is affected by one's own circumstances and one's own perceptions of reality. Though the *fuqahā'* (jurists) tried sincerely to understand the Quranic injunctions, they could understand them only in the light of their own circumstances. Understandings of the divine word can and should change with one's circumstances. In this connection the Qur'ān uses the key word *ma'rūf*, which means "in keeping with the circumstances". The word *ma'ruf* is two-dimensional: one dimension has to do with the social environment, the other with moral and ethical principles. Neither is complete without the other. The moral has to be related with the social.

For this reason *Sharī'ah* was never treated, at least by the earlier jurists, as a closed system. The principle of *ijtihād*, which implies creative interpretation, was incorporated by no less a person than the Prophet himself. The earlier jurists relied on the principle of *ijtihād* in formulating laws, but later the principle of *ijtihād* fell into disuse and the legal corpus of Islam became a closed system. Instead of *ijtihād*, *taqlīd* (imitation) became more acceptable. In the first two centuries of Islam more than a hundred schools of jurisprudence flourished, out of which four main schools survived in Sunnī Islam. This clearly shows the spirit of freedom of thought which characterized the attempt in early Islam to interpret the Quranic verses to develop an Islamic legal system.

***Ḥadīth* literature**

The second important source for the development of legal thought in Islam is *Ḥadīth*, the sayings and doings of the Prophet. No doubt the Prophet was the best person to understand the divine intentions. He could properly interpret the verses and act according to them. Also, he was the guide par excellence for the Muslims, who would go to him and ask questions for guidance in almost all matters. The Prophet either guided them himself or waited for revelation from Allah. When he said or did something it was carefully noted, and his sayings were committed to memory and passed on to others. The Prophet's sayings and doings as recorded in the *Ḥadīth* literature became an important source of legislation in Islam. However, there are two important aspects from which *Ḥadīth* literature needs to be examined: its authenticity and its relation with the Prophet's own epoch.

Many *aḥādīth* (plural of *Ḥadīth*) proliferated after the death of the holy Prophet. The Prophet did not seem enthusiastic about circulation of these sayings; at least he seems not to have encouraged this process. Nor was he keen that people should ask him about everything, for he knew that the coming generations would treat whatever he said as a sacred law. So he often discouraged people from asking questions about their problems. Perhaps the Prophet wanted people to draw more from the Qur'ān by using their rational faculty. The Prophet never asked people to commit his own sayings to memory or to compile them, although he did require people to commit to memory and compile the verses of the Qur'ān, so that nothing would be lost to posterity. Had the *aḥādīth* been as central to the religion of Islam as the Qur'ān, he would have asked the Muslims to commit them to memory and compile them. On the contrary, we find in *Saḥih Muslim* that the Prophet said, "Do not write anything from me except the Qur'ān, and anyone who has written anything other than the Qur'ān should wipe it out."

Some people maintain that this injunction was temporary and that the Prophet later allowed 'Abd Allah Ibn 'Umar to write them down. But this was at best a permission granted to compile the *Ḥadīth* literature, not a necessary requirement. This clearly shows that *aḥādīth* are not an integral part of the formulation of *Sharī'ah*, but at best a complementary factor. And when the Prophet permitted 'Abd Allah Ibn 'Umar to write down *Ḥadīth*, he did not enquire as to which *aḥādīth* he had written down nor did he hear them or correct them, precautions which he did take in the case of the Qur'ān. One can hardly rely on memory for the narration of *Ḥadīth* if it is to be an integral part of or source for Islamic legislation.

The Qur'ān was written down so that there is no controversy about it at all.

Ḥadīth literature has been at the centre of controversy from the very beginning. Its systematic compilation began more than a century after the death of the Prophet, by which time hundreds of thousands of *aḥādīth* were in circulation. A whole science had to be developed to test the authenticity of *Ḥadīth*. The experts developed what was called *'ilm al rijāl* ("science of men"). This attempt to establish the reliability and authenticity of the chain of men narrating the *Ḥadīth* was not a foolproof method, and it was difficult to have a unanimous view about a person's reliability.

Controversies about *aḥādīth* began to develop immediately after the Prophet's death, even though those who had lived with the Prophet were still around. For this reason the first caliph, Abu Bakr, did not permit compilation of *Ḥadīth* either. According to Tadhkirat al Ḥuffāẓ, Imām Dhahabī said that, after the death of the Prophet, Abu Bakr gathered together all the people and said,

> You ascribe *Ḥadīth* to the Apostle of Allah and then differ with each other about them. Those who come after you will differ even more intensely with each other. So it is desirable not to ascribe things to the Prophet. And if anyone enquires about it, you should say that between you is the Book of Allah, and whatever has been permitted by it should be permissible and whatever has been prohibited by it should be prohibited.

The same thing is said about 'Umar, the second caliph. When he consulted people about *Ḥadīth*, they opined that it should be compiled. But 'Umar was not satisfied with this opinion. For a whole month he went on thinking about it, and one morning, with great concentration of mind, he came to the conclusion that it should *not* be compiled. He told people, "I had thought about compiling *Ḥadīth* but then it occurred to me that the people before us also compiled books and resorted to them and ignored the Book of Allah and, by Allah, I do not want that anything else be mixed up with the Book of Allah." When the *Ḥadīth* literature proliferated anyway during 'Umar's time, he ordered, according to Ṭabaqāt Ibn Sa'd, all compilations to be brought before him and issued orders to burn them.

The fear that forged *Ḥadīth* would soon multiply and people would give more importance to them than to the Qur'ān was not unfounded. Despite the stringent measures by the Prophet and the caliphs, *Ḥadīth* multiplied exponentially. During Imam Mālik's time (died 179 A.H.)

there were no more than a few hundred *Ḥadīth* (in his *Mutawātir* there are no more than 300 to 500 *aḥādīth*); by the time of Imām Bukhārī (died 256 A.H.) his collection came to more than 600,000 — of which he selected no more than 2630 *Ḥadīth* in all. Among the Sunnī Muslims there are six authentic collections of *Ḥadīth* known as the *Ṣiḥah Sittah*. Besides these, there are those collected by the Shi'ah Muslims, for whom the *Ṣiḥah Sittah* are not reliable. Similarly for the Sunnī the Shi'ah collections are not reliable.

To expect that whatever the holy Prophet said would remain undistorted would be to expect the impossible, even if no one's integrity in the chain of narrators were doubted. This was not so. Vested interests led some people to coin spurious *Ḥadīth* for their own legitimation. Forging *Ḥadīth* became a flourishing industry as different interests used so-called sayings of the Prophet for their own use. The rulers also were in great need of *Ḥadīth* literature. Rival factions struggling for power wanted legitimation for their deviations through sayings of the Prophet, and there are many examples of this in the *Ḥadīth* literature.

It is thus extremely problematic to accept the entire *Ḥadīth* literature as authentic. Many problems arise even with respect to the six authentic compilations. The Ḥanafī Muslims consider about 200 *Ḥadīth* from Bukhārī as problematic. But even if the entire *Ṣiḥāh Sittah* is considered quite authentic, problems of a different nature arise. The Qur'ān itself includes verses which are contextual. They were revealed in a certain context and had validity in that context. For example, the Qur'ān requires a portion of *zakāt* to be spent on what it calls *al mu‘allafat qulūbuhum* for winning the hearts of non-Muslims who allied themselves with the Muslims. Hazrat ‘Umar stopped spending a portion of *zakāt* on this category, arguing that Islam was by then strong enough and did not need support from anyone else. Thus with the change of context the applicability of the Quranic verse on *zakāt* changed.

One can also give an example in the context of *Ḥadīth*. We read in one of the *Ḥadīth* (in Sunan Abi Dāwūd) that the holy Prophet strongly condemned the pronouncement of triple divorce in one sitting and asked the man who had pronounced it to take back his wife. Thus, according to this *Ḥadīth*, triple divorce in one sitting is strongly prohibited. But in a changed context, Hazrat ‘Umar enforced it again; and since then, though called *ṭalāq al-bida‘*, "innovated" or "sinful" form of divorce, it is considered valid. In the case of *Ḥadīth*, then, context matters. In fact, *Ḥadīth* represents the contextual application of the Qur'ān. If *Ḥadīth* is the sayings and doings of the Prophet, it has a contextual dimension. The

Prophet, through his sayings and doings, tried to apply the teachings of the Qur'ān to his own times.

Even the normative aspects of scriptural teachings have to be imparted a contextual dimension in order to make them effective for and acceptable to the people of a particular era. The Prophet lived among Arabs who had their own ethos, customs, traditions, civilization and economic compulsions, which had to be kept in view when applying the Quranic teachings. Islam as represented by Quranic values and norms had great revolutionary potential, but not all of this could be actualized in the given Arab context. A reformer or revolutionary cannot ignore altogether the given context and the received traditions. The Prophet had to make certain concessions in view of the society he lived in while applying the Quranic teachings. Thus *Ḥadīth*, even if most authentic, cannot be an eternal component of *Sharī'ah*.

This discussion can be illustrated by a few examples. The Qur'ān declares in one of its verses: "And surely we have honoured the children of Adam" (17:70). It is evident that "children of Adam" includes all humans, without any distinction, including that of master and slave. All have been honoured, and all are equal in the eyes of Allah. This was a great revolutionary ideal, upholding the equality of all human beings by making them equally respectable in the eyes of Allah. However, in view of the prevailing conditions such equality could not be achieved, and Islam had to permit slavery, albeit reluctantly and with an effort at easing the conditions of their life. The elevated principle of equality had to be toned down in view of the concrete conditions. The true potentialities of Islamic teachings could not be realized.

The question of sexual equality falls into the same category. The real intention of the Qur'ān was to accord equal status to both sexes. Women, like men, are human beings, and all human beings are equally honourable in the eyes of Allah. Furthermore, the Qur'ān also separately declared the principle of equality of sexes, *wa lahunna mithl al-ladhi 'alayhinna* ("women's rights are the same as their obligation in a just manner") (2:228). But in view of the prevailing conditions and social context, sexual equality was not achievable, so the Qur'ān had to add: "and men are a degree above them". Without men being given a slightly upper hand, the Islamic ideal of equality would not have been accepted in that society. Although the Quranic norm was equality of sexes, men forged many *Ḥadīth* giving women far more inferior status. Thus the *Sharī'ah* which based its laws on these *aḥādīth* in respect of women will have to be rethought in the changed context. Polygamy was also a contextual provision in the Qur’ān. It cannot be treated as eternal privilege by men, nor an unrestricted one. If the *Sharī‘ah* positions are rethought suitably in today’s context, the great Islamic ideal of equality of sexes can be realized.

Ijmā‘ (consensus)

The concept of *ijmā‘* (consensus) implies that if there is consensus of the community on crucial issues it will become an integral part of Islamic *Sharī‘ah*. When the great jurists agree unanimously on an issue, it is known as *ijma‘ ḥaqīqī*; when a few jurists agree with each other while others remain silent (in other words, do not oppose one formulation), it is called *ijma‘ sukūtū* (silent consensus). The second category is also treated as the consensus of the whole community. Some go to the extent of saying that one who rejects *ijmā‘* (*ḥaqīqī* or *sukūtū*) is a *kāfir*, a renouncer of Islam or an atheist. Some even take the extreme position that such people must be punished by death.

It must be understood that *ijmā‘* is merely a tertiary source and cannot be as binding as the Qur’ān or Sunnah, which have much more elevated status. In other words, the opinion of some or most of the Islamic jurists cannot become what is called *ḥujjāt al-shar‘* (the proof of part of *Sharī‘ah*). Al ‘Allamah Shawh‘ānī points out in his book *Irshād al-Fuḥūl* that *ijmā‘* cannot stand by itself but must be based on the Qur’ān or Sunnah. ‘Allamah Ibn Ḥazm makes a similar point in his book *Kitāb al-Aḥkām*. Thus *ijmā‘* by itself obviously cannot become a source of Islamic law, as is often mistakenly thought; those who resort to *ijmā‘* must also cite proof from the Qur’ān or Sunnah.

But if *ijmā‘* by itself cannot assume central significance, this does not mean that it has no role to play. Intelligently and creatively used, it can play an important role in modern Islamic legislation. The noted Islamic thinker and poet Iqbal, in his *Reconstruction of Religious Thought in Islam,* has pointed out that a modern parliament in an Islamic country may constitute a body which can play the role of *ijmā‘*. This raises the important question of whether such a body can bring about changes in the *Sharī‘ah* codified by the great jurists.

We have already pointed out that *Sharī‘ah* is not and should not be treated as a closed system. Its dynamism and vitality depend on its capacity to change with the times. Of course these changes will not be in principles and values but in their proper application, keeping in view the social and other contexts. The *aḥkām shar‘iyyah* (injunctions) change with space, time and social conditions. During the period of the holy

Prophet, Hazrat 'Umar changed many decisions taken by the Prophet. If the rightly guided caliphs could change the injunctions of the Qur'ān and Sunnah even though they were so close to the period of the Prophet, why may we not make changes more than 1400 years later? Ibn Qayyim Al Jūziyyah, a noted disciple of the great Islamic thinker Ibn Taymiyyah, points out that the *Sharī'ah* is not meant for creating difficulties and problems but is rather based on the welfare of the people in the matters of this life and the life hereafter. Thus *Sharī'ah* is the embodiment of justice, mercy, welfare and wisdom. Something that becomes its opposite — oppression, cruelty, mischief and absurdity — cannot be called *Sharī'ah*.

It was in this spirit that Hazrat 'Umar took many decisions which were apparently contradictory to the Qur'ān and Sunnah but in fact were not. He suspended the punishment of cutting off hands for theft during famine; he again enforced the triple *ṭalāq* (on account of its misuse by Arabs after the conquest of Syria, Egypt, Persia, etc.); he stopped the sale of slave girls; he did not distribute the lands conquered by the Muslims (though both the Qur'ān and Sunnah allowed it); he stopped giving a portion of *zakāt* to the allies of Muslims (*al mu'allafat qulūbuhum*); he changed the punishment for fornication (that is, suspended the practice of externment for one year though continued the one hundred lashes). For all these decisions there were very good reasons. He was not violating the real intention behind the *aḥkām*; rather, since their objectives were not being achieved in the new situation, he effected changes in them. It was for this reason that Imām Ibn Taymiyyah prescribed the famous doctrine that with the change of times the injunctions change (*taghayyur al aḥkām bi taghayyur al azmān*). Maulana 'Alā'ī also points out that because the *shar'ī* injunctions are based on causes, when the causes change, the injunctions also change.

A study of the process of evolution in the different schools of Islamic jurisprudence (Mālikī, Ḥanbalī, Ḥanafī and Shāfi'ī) shows that their formulations were greatly affected by their own social, cultural and economic conditions. The differences in their formulations were precisely due to differing conditions. *Sharī'ah* should be considered as an attempt to achieve Quranic goals, values and principles. It is a means, not an end. Unfortunately, it is often considered an end in itself, and this approach creates many problems. The growth of the *Sharī'ah* has stopped because of such rigid attitudes towards it. It has become stagnant. Despite a plethora of examples that the great classical jurists of Islam had an open mind on *shar'ī* issues, our *'ulamā'* and jurists have a totally closed mind. They indulge only in *taqlīd* (imitation) and any rethinking is considered nothing less than sin and *kufr*. The Shah Bano movement in India was product of such a mindset. The continuation of triple *talāq* is also a result of such stagnant thinking.

It is unfortunate that no Muslim country has taken a lead in this matter. Those who have come to be known as fundamentalists want to apply *Sharī'ah* mechanically and unthinkingly. They refuse to take modern conditions into account. It would be of great benefit to all those who treat *Sharī'ah* as immutable to study the history of evolution of various schools of *Sharī'ah*. Without the creative spirit of *ijtihād*, *Sharī'ah* cannot play a useful role in modern times.

6. Notes on *Sharī'ah*, *Fiqh* and *Ijtihād*

MOKHTAR IHSAN AZIZ

To accept the premise that the divine texts are binding on us while our own interpretations and independent endeavours to explain them are not is in my opinion the shortest way to creating adequate rapport between Islam and Christianity.

One of the main axioms of belief in Islam is the unity of heavenly messages, since despite their variety they emanate in essence from one source. God Almighty says, "He has ordained for you the faith which He enjoined on Nuh and which we have revealed to you, and which we enjoined on Ibrahim, Musa and Isa, saying, 'Observe this faith and be not divided therein'" (Sūrat al-Shūra; 42:13). A second fact is that difference in religion occurs by the will of God. God Almighty says, "Had your Lord pleased, all the people of the earth would have believed in him. Would you then force men to be believers?" (Sūrat Yūnis; 10:99). Therefore, Muslims are not enjoined to hold other people accountable for their beliefs but are to restrict their efforts to conveying God's word only. "If they turn away, know that we have not sent you to be their keeper, your only duty is to warn them" (Sūrat al-Shūra; 42:48).

The method of dealing with the People of the Book is defined by the Qur'ān as follows: "And do not argue with the People of the Book except in the best way, unless it be with those among them who do evil. Say, 'We believe in that which is revealed to us and which was revealed to you. Our God and your God is one. To him we surrender ourselves'" (Sūrat al-'Ankabūt; 29:46).

These basic pillars of belief no doubt play an important role in the psychological and cultural formation of the Muslim individual and serve as basis for his stands and attitude towards himself, his community and others. These, I believe, have not stirred any arguments. The arguments revolve around the enormous amount of *ijtihād*, interpretations and *fiqh*, which in its entirety is no more than a human creative effort that has interacted with the challenges and novel circumstances of specific times and places in order to seek solutions to problems or to elicit legal judgments in accordance with the methods of the fundamentalists, which are geared for the realization of the overall intentions of the *Sharīʻah*. Even though this is complementary to the revelations, it has no absolute validity but is restricted by the circumstances of the specific times and places.

It may be appropriate at this point to look at some of the idioms and concepts pertaining to relations between Muslims and non-Muslims within and outside Islamic society. It should be pointed out, for example, that the idiom "the abode of war and the abode of Islam" (*Dār al-Ḥarb wa Dār al-Islām*), which is prevalent in our *fiqh* heritage, has no origin in the *Sharīʻah* but is purely the work of the *fuqahā'* in the context of their descriptions of the political and life realities of their times. The fact is that Islam did not come to wage war and never initiated it, resorting to it only against those who fought it or took a hostile stance against Islam. The rule in Muslim relationships with others is peace, and war is the exception. This is the opinion of the great majority of Muslim jurists. Good references on this matter can be found in the grand Sira (the life of the prophet) interpretation with commentaries by Professor Abu Zahra, and in "The Provisions of International Law in the Islamic *Sharīʻah*" by Dr Ḥāmid Sultan.

This type of *ijtihād* in *fiqh* regarding international relationships did indeed stir some polemics from the point of view of the *fuqahā'* who advocated the division of *Dār al-Islām* and *Dār al-Ḥarb*. Some saw in this advocacy an abandonment of the high values confirmed by Islam, such as the protection of virtues, freedoms and justice. But those *fuqahā'* who advocated the division could not help calling things by their names, since war was a reality of their times. In any case, this was the opinion of a minority at a particular time, not one of the pillars of religion. In the framework of the objective historical realities of this context, we can understand the *dhimmah* contract. Linguistically, *dhimmah* means a pledge of security, and to the *fuqahā'* the *dhimmah* contract is a commitment to "settle them in our abodes, protect them and safeguard them, and they in turn pay the *jizyah* or choose to enter Islam". Therefore the Quranic verse which says, "until they pay the *jizyah* out of hand and are utterly subdued" means that *jizyah* is the most that is asked of the fighters surrendering to the Muslims. As for the *dhimmi*, he is the fighter who chooses to refrain from the defence of God's cause but wants to reside in the Muslim abodes on condition that he be treated the same as Muslims in terms of rights and duties. The *dhimmah* contract is distinguished from the ordinary pledge of security or *amān* in that the latter can be given by any ordinary Muslim while the former must be given by the imām or general authority. Moreover, *dhimmah* is an eternal contract which applies as well to the individual's descendants after him. *Fuqahā'* are unanimous in their opinion that two conditions must be fulfilled to meet the prerequisites for the eternal *dhimmah* contract: (1) able-bodied *dhimmiyūn* must commit themselves to contributing to the costs and general budget of the state; (2) *dhimmiyūn* must abide by Islamic regulations in financial matters and social relations. As for family matters, such as marriage and divorce and their consequences, it is well established in *fiqh* and in actual historical experience that *dhimmiyīn* are free to apply their own creeds. The *fiqh* axiom, "We are commanded to leave them [*dhimmiyīn*] to their own beliefs", is a confirmation of the right of religious freedom for the *dhimmiyīn*.

In fact, the Ḥanafī *fuqahā'* went even further: they permitted the *dhimmiyīn* to drink alcohol and eat pork if that is permitted in their creeds, in order to avoid any interference in their personal freedoms. Moreover, if a Muslim spilled the wine or killed a pig belonging to a *dhimmi*, he must pay compensation for that, while if the opposite happened the *dhimmi* is not required to pay because wine and pigs are not of value to a Muslim. Perhaps these examples provide an adequate answer to the question of whether the application of *Sharī'ah* contradicts the plurality of laws within an Islamic state.

But does the concept of the *dhimmah* contract coincide with what we call in contemporary political expression the right of citizenship? In my opinion the answer is No. Details on this can be found in Professor Fahmī Huwaydī's book *Citizens not Dhimmis*. The *fuqahā'* maintain that sovereignty and authority in the Islamic state belongs to the *shar'ī* or canonic law and nowhere else. Policy-making therefore may not deviate from its rules and provisions, or from what Al Imām al Ghazālī calls "the laws of policy", which Ibn Khaldūn defines as "forcing people to abide by the requirements of the canonic law to safeguard the religion and manage worldly affairs through it". This is equivalent to the "high authority or legitimacy" or "the dominance of the law" in the language of the contemporaries. Professor Muhammad Durcini says in his book *Studies and Researches in Contemporary Islamic Thought*, in a discussion of the matter of sovereignty, "It is unimaginable in the Islamic creed to have a policy which neglects the rules of religion and its provisions, ways and intentions, for these are the pillars of sovereignty in the state." It is important here to make a distinction between the sovereignty of the canonic law and that of the general authority which undertakes the execution of these laws in the practical life of people. Power and infallibility belong to the *Sharīʻah* and are not extended to the general authority whose duty is to guard and implement the *Sharīʻah*. General authority in Islam is the right of the nation, which it assumes and manages in such a way as to realize its interests.

I want to underline here the importance of the distinction between Islamic *Sharīʻah* and Islamic *fiqh*. We must distinguish between the solid and invariable divine provisions and the changing social and historical *ijtihād* of the *fuqahā'*. Professor Justice Ṭariq al-Bishrī maintains that this is "our recourse to acquiring the ability to preserve the fundamentals of *Sharīʻah* and at the same time use our minds in the vast realm of *ijtihād*, so that we may preserve the *Sharīʻah*, safeguard the interests of the people and spread justice among them. The realm of *ijtihād* is the social and historical realm in Islamic thought and its *fiqh*. Here a connection must be made between the intellectual solutions and their social functions and it should be based on the intentions of the Islamic *Sharīʻah*, namely the preservation of religion and safeguarding of the Islamic community and protection of the minds, honour and possessions."

Indeed, the renewal and revival of Islamic *fiqh* entails connecting it with the reality of life, and this in turn entails its strengthening in the land. This is the way to achieve harmony between the social reality, its institutions, relationships and models of behaviour and the provisions and ideas of *fiqh*. Integration and bonds are thus established between religious science and world science, between practical life and the life of worship.

Part II

7. On the Urgency of *Ijtihād*

KHALID ZIADEH

The debate on religion and state in the Muslim world has taken a new turn in the last two decades of this century.

Notwithstanding the various affirmations among Islamists and their opponents alike, this debate cannot — and does not as a matter of fact — return to the past. The discourse we analyze is only partially a reproduction of a traditional one. Modern nationalism and the political, social and cultural effects of secularization in Muslim societies raise a new set of issues.

The role of the state in relation to society needs to be examined as we look at the Islamist ideological mobilization. Throughout the first two-thirds of this century, *Sharī'ah* was generally confined to family law. Ruling elites were overwhelmingly preoccupied with building up viable national states. Adoption of legal systems was a function of this preoccupation and was not on the whole an object of a passionate controversy, since the problems at the heart of political life focused on independence, national unity and social and economic progress. But issues relevant to the question of identity were lively. In the search for *aṣālah* (authenticity) in opposition to Western cultural domination, Islam was indeed an active principle, a sort of driving force. The passionate reference to the *turāth* (cultural heritage) revealed the strength of a not necessarily political Islamic self-assertion.

It is only when the promises of national states and nationalist projects to achieve liberation and development did not come true that the affirmation of Islamic identity was forcefully politicized. Abiding by *Sharī'ah* then became first and foremost a condition for a legitimate state. The call for Islamic rule functions, undoubtedly, as a protest against illegitimate tyranny.

The Islamicization of life was no longer bound to the individual and social moral realm but rather viewed as an all-embracing, but primarily political ideal. The upsurge of Islamism and religious revival, though apparently connected, should not be confused.

Instead of drawing on the historical experience of Muslims and their *fuqahā'*, the Islamist movements opted for "going back to the origins", claiming to model the state on that of the Prophet. They could not be reconciled to the fact that Muslim scholars accepted partial applications of *Sharī'ah* and did in fact justify the existence of different patterns of Muslim governance which were not strictly "Islamic". Moreover, Islamic jurisprudence was elaborated outside the state, and Muslims were often willing to honour it, irrespective of the governments' authority. One could say, furthermore, that Muslims accepted some form of separation between *Sharī'ah* and the state.

This brings us to the complex but crucial discussion of the modes of interaction between religion and state. Far be it from us to deny that there is a specific Islamic approach to this question. Islam, it is often said, is *Dīn* (religion) and *Dawlah* (state). The significance of the "and" is not always self-evident.

We also know that comparing Christianity and Islam is not as simple as some secularists, including Christians, suggest. Western and "Christian" societies do not obey the imperatives of a radical separation of realms. Religion is not entirely privatized, nor spiritualized, as often conveyed in the traditional Muslim — and to some extent Christian — understanding of secularization. The role of religion and religious institutions in education is just one case in point.

Concerning modernization, we should not ignore the distinction between the social process and the political expressions, more particularly those pertaining to state structures and laws. Nor should we forget that modernization in the Muslim world was initiated "from above", by the rulers of Ottoman Turkey and Egypt. It too was brought in from "abroad".

The rejection of modernity is a rejection of the state that imposed it and expresses an opposition to Western hegemony. Nevertheless, re-affirming the Islamic personality against intruding influences cannot overshadow the real changes that have affected traditional Muslim societies. Voluntarist claims should not, and cannot, obscure historical mutations.

There is no harm in re-emphasizing the urgency of *ijtihād*. The question of co-citizenship, beyond what is stipulated in the *dhimmah* pact, illustrates what avenues are to be opened and were indeed opened for creative *fiqhi* thinking or reinterpretation. Many other contemporary issues invite similar efforts. The status of Muslims who are permanently living in non-Muslim societies is one example that concerns us directly in our Muslim-Christian dialogue.

New situations and the way to cope with them await an innovative "theoretical" reflection. We cannot leave the historical accommodations that Muslims were forced, or chose, to make, outside the sphere of Islamic thought. It is certainly the responsibility of *fuqahā'*, but not theirs only.

8. *Sharī'ah* and Religious Pluralism

BERT F. BREINER

The road to *falāḥ*

The English "Islamic law" does not adequately capture the connotations of the Arabic *Sharī'ah*, either etymologically or semantically. Etymologically, the word is related to the concept of "way" or "path", and Arabic lexicographers indicate that it more specifically refers to "path to water".[1] It is not difficult to see in the meaning "path to water" a reference to the *Sharī'ah* as a "path to life" — or, perhaps better, the "road to *falāḥ*" ("success in this world and the next"). Since the translation "success in this world and the next" is awkward, I prefer "self-fulfilment" or "human fulfilment", in the sense that *falāḥ* denotes the fulfilment of the true goal of human life.

In this context, however, "success in this world and the next" will help to highlight some of the points I would like to make about the *Sharī'ah*. First, this translation focuses attention on an important respect in which the Muslim understanding of *Sharī'ah* (as, incidentally, the Jewish understanding of Torah) differs from Christian understandings of "law". No Christian thinker would ever describe law as the "way to success in this world and the next"; even less would a Christian writer describe law in any form as the "way to salvation", to use a more specifically Christian vocabulary. Since it is not my purpose here to compare Christian and Muslim understandings of law, I will not go further into the Christian understanding of law, its history or its relationship to Christian theology. But this difference is important. If *Sharī'ah* may be seen in its broadest sense as the "way which leads to *falāḥ*/success in this world and the next", no Christian could ever have developed such a formulation about law in any sense.

This also explains how *Sharī'ah* is broader than the Western (and, to a lesser extent, the Christian) understanding of law. There are frequently sections in books on *Sharīʻah* which deal with *adab*, often translated in this context as "ethics". Many prescriptions, both positive and negative, may be found in the *Sharīʻah* which are not intended to be legally enforceable. In fact, the *fuqahā'* (Islamic jurists) have generally classified all actions into five categories ranging from absolutely required to absolutely forbidden. This whole gamut of possibilities is contained within the *Sharīʻah*, whereas a Western understanding of law would generally exclude all aspects of such a system which are not subject to any kind of legal enforcement.

This does not mean *Sharīʻah* = law + ethics. There is a rich literature of philosophical ethics in Islam (*al-falsafah al-adabiyyah*) which is definitely *not* part of the *Sharīʻah* literature. The problem is that Islam and Western thought are working with different concepts which do not correspond. The criteria by which Western thinkers usually distinguish between law and ethics are not applicable to a discussion of *Sharīʻah*. Generally in the West a precept which is not enforceable is not a "law" but "ethics". In Islam, precepts which can be immediately derived according to recognized rules of reasoning from the Qur'ān and the Sunnah (practice and teaching of the Prophet Muḥammad) are *Sharīʻah* in the broadest sense, whether or not they are legally enforceable. This enables a number of Muslim thinkers to make a meaningful distinction between *Sharīʻah* and *fiqh* — the latter being the whole of Islamic jurisprudence, the theory and codification of Islamic law.

Nevertheless, there is always a legal dimension to the *Sharīʻah*: it is the way to *falāḥ*, success in this world and the next. In one sense, the way to *falāḥ* is the "righteous will of God" or, from the human perspective, "justice" (*ʻadl*). The Qur'an is one with the Hebrew prophets of the Bible in stressing God's concern for justice. Sūrat al-Māʻun (107) expresses the same concern for justice in society which we read in the biblical Psalms and prophets (e.g., Ps. 10; Isa. 56:1-2; Jer. 8:4-17; Ezek. 7:10; Amos 5; Micah 3). Even more to the point are verses like Surat al-Nisā' (4:125), which urges Muslims to be just "even though it be against yourselves or your parents or your kindred", or Sūrat al-Mā'idah (5:8): "be steadfast witnesses for God in equity, and do not let hatred of any people seduce you so that you do not deal justly".

The intention of this comparison between the Qur'ān and the Hebrew prophets is to point to the concern of the latter for "justice in the gate" (cf. Amos 5:15), in other words, for the public administration of justice, not simply or even primarily for moral action on the part of individuals. This is a crucial point: God cares passionately about justice, which means a divine concern for a just social structure. A just social structure is of course broader than a just political structure. But that is precisely the point: that it is broader not narrower implies a divine concern for and active interest in the question of political structures.

Individual and community

Islamic faith and practice have much to say to a society struggling with the relationship between the individual and the community. I think this struggle is happening in the secularized West, although it would be too simplistic to say that the West is fundamentally "individualistic". It is useful to remember that secular humanists (indeed often Marxist atheists) have done more to highlight the *communal* structures of injustice than have traditional religious systems — including Islam, which has however gone much further in this direction than Christianity has. It is largely to secular humanists that we owe much of the current awareness of the global, national and corporate dimensions of economic injustice. Yet, although it may be inaccurate simply to label secular humanist thought as "individualistic", it does have serious problems in dealing with the relationship between the individual and the community. For example, I detect a growing disenchantment with the adequacy of "voluntary organizations", important as they are, to deal with the problem of the relationship between the individual and the community, in part because they are themselves subject to all the forces of a poorly regulated market economy.

Some of the principles which arise in this discussion challenge my long-cherished Western assumptions. For example, I now consider it an open question whether a secular democracy offers an intrinsically better safeguard of human rights than a religious state. I realize this verges on "heresy" in terms of modern Western orthodoxy, but let me explain by giving an example. Malaysia has a secular constitution which recognizes Islam as the official religion. Constitutionally, it is a secular democracy. There is also in Malaysia a series of laws (which vary from state to state) prohibiting Christians from using certain "Islamic terms" when they worship in the national language, chief among them *Allah*. It is unlikely that such a restriction on non-Muslim worship (particularly for Christians and Jews) could be justified or even permitted under the classical formulations of Islamic *fiqh*. Christians and Jewish Arabs, for example, have worshipped God as Allah since before the coming of the Prophet, and their right to do so has never been challenged by Islamic legal theory. Malaysia, however, is a secular state, and in its effort to protect the interest of Islam it is ironically not bound by the formulations and principles of Islamic law. Here we are speaking about the "will of the majority" and not about the "law of God". The result is a restriction on the rights of non-Muslims, promulgated to protect the interests of Islam, which Islamic law itself would not countenance.

Of course, Western legal theory does in principle impose limits to the sovereign will of the majority and is justly proud of its role in developing and defending the modern concept of human rights. In some cases these rights are enshrined in law in a form similar to the United States Bill of Rights. They tend, however, to stress the rights of *individuals* and only rarely deal with the rights of minorities *as groups*. The importance of the communal dimension is becoming painfully clear in many situations about which we read daily in the newspapers. This does not mean that Western law is unable to recognize the legal position of a group as opposed to an individual — there are laws about race relations in many Western countries and the concept of a class-action suit is well established, at least in US legal practice — but the primary emphasis remains on the rights of individuals, and the law seeks to ensure that persons do not suffer as *individuals* because of their belonging to a particular group. Moreover, the rights and duties of groups is a comparatively marginal and poorly integrated aspect of Western legal thinking. Indeed, the legal fiction of the "corporate personality" emphasizes a natural tendency in Western law to conceptualize the application of rights and duties primarily in terms of individuals.

The creation of a genuinely pluralist society, whether within the territory of a particular sovereign state or on a more global level, requires that the reality of group identity and cohesion be well integrated into the legal system. In this respect, the classical formulation of the *Sharī'ah* may well have more to offer the development of a just and pluralist society than many principles enshrined in Western secular law. Before developing these principles as points for discussion, however, it is important to remember that many of them were subjected to severe restrictions (to our modern way of thinking) by many of the classical *fuqahā'*. That is, however, all the more reason for suggesting that genuine dialogue on these principles is crucial for Christian-Muslim relations today. In fact it could be argued that the principles which lay behind the Islamic legal understanding of communal identity highlight areas of urgent concern not only for Christians and Muslims but for any global quest for a just pluralism in the modern world.

Communalism and pluralism: three principles

There are, I believe, three principles derivable from classical *fiqh* which have a direct bearing on the question of communalism and pluralism in society and in law. The first is the theoretical relationship between the individual and the community. Every individual is a member of a community; ultimately, however, he or she is this by choice and by right. Immediately this raises a thorny issue. Classical *fiqh* severely limited this right by making apostasy from Islam punishable by death (unless you happened to be a woman belonging to the Ḥanafī school of law). Some legal theorists even disallowed change of religion on the part of non-Muslims (unless it was a question of conversion to Islam). Today there is a great deal of discussion about this point among Muslims. Many would argue that the precedent for this penalty in the Sunnah really applied to treason, and that in a different historical context it need not, indeed should not, apply to apostasy per se. They argue that the only punishment for apostasy stipulated in the Qur'ān is hellfire.[2]

While the specific application of this freedom needs urgent discussion, it is the principle that I want to highlight here. Every individual is a member of a community, but he or she has the right to choose the community to which he or she belongs. That human existence is essentially and fundamentally communal is a matter of common sense: no one could survive infancy without some community, upon which he or she is totally dependent for the first several years of life. But it is also a matter of sound sociology and psychology, though sometimes hidden behind the jargon of "peer groups", "subcultures", "group identification" and the "socialization process". That each individual has the right to choose his or her community is consonant with Western and Christian ideas of individual freedom. In fact, this freedom has been taken further, again as a principle, in Islamic law. We find this in an important corollary to which we shall return shortly: the right of a person to be judged according to the faith and practice of his or her own community.

The second major principle is that within one social organization a plurality of legal systems may be applied. Although this contrasts sharply with the contemporary Western understanding of law, which I shall call "secular humanist", it has not always been the case in the history of European law. Roman law, at least until citizenship was granted to most inhabitants of the Roman provinces, knew the concept of a plurality of legal systems within one jurisdiction, and this principle was adopted by the Eastern Roman or Byzantine legal codes. Generally this served to restrict the rights of Jews and heretics rather than to protect them — but not always. It was also the norm in Western Europe, at least through the early Middle Ages. In contemporary Western secular thought, however, equality before the law generally means that one and the same law is applied to all, without discrimination on the basis of race, religion, language, sex or class. There are, of course, some exceptions and many of these relate to freedom of conscience, which includes, but is not limited to, the freedom to practice one's religion. Traditionally, however, this is formulated as a right of the individual and is understood in any case as a right *within* the prevailing legal system rather than the right to a parallel legal system within the same jurisdiction.

The area in which Western legal theory most readily recognizes the possible validity of parallel jurisdictions is international law. In particular, there is great deal of discussion about the law of personal status. Even so, the tendency in Western law is to a uniformity of law within one political entity. An interesting historical example, dealing precisely with the law of personal status, is the discussion of polygamy which accompanied the process by which predominantly Mormon Utah became a state rather than a territory of the United States.

Discussions about introducing Islamic personal law are so controversial in the West because the experience of the application of different laws of personal status is virtually limited to places which have some kind of Islamic legal influence in their history. Thus from North Africa through the Middle East and the Indian subcontinent to Southeast Asia there is a large band of countries which generally recognize the right of different communities to marry, divorce, inherit and adopt children according to their own religious law. In these matters, different laws apply to different religious communities, and there is often a parallel civil code as well, which may be applied to those who do not belong to any recognized religious community or wish to have their affairs decided according to a secular legal system rather than that of their religious community.

The third principle is the personal application of law: the fact that a person is judged according to the law of the community he or she has chosen. In principle both Muslims and non-Muslims have the right to be judged according to the law of their own community. In other words, Muslim law is a law essentially of personal/communal application rather than a law of territorial application as is the theory of modern Western law. This is again a matter of interpretation. Discussing the competence of Muslim and non-Muslim courts in Islamic legal theory, Fattal argues that Ḥanafī law, as opposed to the other Sunnī *madhāhib* (schools of law), has a strong territorial concept, in seeing Muslim courts as the normal place of adjudication for all people living under Muslim jurisdiction (except in matters which are *ḥarām* for Muslims, such as wine and pork).[3] This perception, however, may reflect a confusion of the concepts of territory and society. Rather, I think we have in Abū Ḥanifah a weak echo of the Pact of Al Madīnah, in which the Prophet Muḥammad said of Muslim and non-Muslim together that they were *ummattun wāḥidatun*, one people.[4] To the best of my knowledge this phrase (and perhaps this sentiment) was lost in Islamic legal theory until it reappeared in the preamble to "The Sudan Charter"[5], to which we shall return shortly. However, it is clear from the text of the Pact of Al Madīnah and subsequent Muslim legal theory that "one people" does not mean "one law" in the sense of total uniformity.

Again there are complications in the way classical *fiqh* has applied this principle. In terms of the relationships between the *madhahib*, there are questions of *taqlīd* (following the received tradition) and *takhayyur* (combining or mixing rulings from different law schools). In terms of our topic, there are serious restrictions on the principle of the personal application of law. The first is the vexed question of *ḥudūd*. For Al Shāfi'ī and Ibn Ḥanbal these were applicable to non-Muslims; for Abū Ḥanifah and Mālik, since non-Muslims were not considered *muḥṣan* (legally competent and responsible), *ḥadd* punishments did not apply to them, and when they were applied, as in the case of theft, it was because the crime was considered *fasād fi al-'ard* (literally, "corrupting the earth").

More important was the question of the court of competence, especially in cases where the parties involved represented different communities. In fact, studies of the Ottoman sijills show that non-Muslims often chose the Muslim court even when this was not necessary. The major problem here is one of procedure. Islamic law relies heavily on the testimony of witnesses, and non-Muslims were theoretically not recognized as valid witnesses against Muslims (with an exception in Ḥanbalī law in cases of inheritance). Abū Ḥanifah, however, allowed non-Muslims to testify in cases that did not involve a Muslim, and this became the Ottoman practice. In fact, the sijills show that non-Muslims were accepted as witnesses on behalf of Muslims or corroborating a Muslim witness.[6]

The status of non-Muslims as witnesses in classical *fiqh* is, of course, based on the interpretation of the classical jurists, and some divergent opinions exist in more modern times. Shaykh Shaltūt, a former *shaykh al-Azhar*, writes in his book comparing the law schools that this rule was historically conditioned and need not apply today, though he does not develop this remark. I assume, however, that all such *fiqh* rules are open to a new *ijtihād* (literally, "effort, struggle"; the term refers to the process of Islamic legal codification of *fiqh*).

I believe these principles make Islamic law a potentially excellent basis for developing a pluralistic society. But they would obviously require a new *ijtihād* in the specifics. Unfortunately, many attempts to update Islamic law end up compromising rather than developing these principles of classical Islamic law. An excellent example is the Sudan Charter, which as we have seen echoes the sentiments of the Pact of Al Madīnah in its opening words. It is clearly an attempt to be open and accommodating in the interests of peace. In it we read that "the Sudan does not conform to the doctrine of centralism or absolute universality of law...; the scope of some laws can be limited as to particular persons or places".[7] This seems an excellent illustration of what I have identified as basic principles of Islamic law, except for the reference to places. What happens is that "family law shall be personal"; in other cases, however, "the effectiveness of some laws shall be subject to territorial limitations".[8]

This document is important because it clearly shows a willingness to develop Islamic law in the service of a genuine pluralism. But there are perhaps other developments of Islamic law which would provide an even more solid basis for a pluralistic society. And it is this possibility I would like to see Christians and Muslims talk about together much more.

There are, then, three principles of Islamic legal theory which ought to be discussed in the contemporary search for a just basis for a genuinely pluralist society: the personal rather than territorial application of law, the communal nature of law (including the right of different communities to formulate their own law) and freedom of choice in terms of communal affiliation, with the concomitant right to be judged according to one's own community's system of law.

Intercommunal jurisdiction

A number of problems remain, most obviously that of intercommunal jurisdiction. Part of the problem here is to agree on the judicial procedure to be used — for example, witnesses or forensic evidence. This is not just a matter of a study of comparative law, but would involve some serious discussion and research into the value and ethics of different forms of judicial proof. It is not possible simply to assume that contemporary Western judicial procedure is based on a more equitable system of justice than the classical Islamic one. Questions such as the rights of the accused need to be examined openly and critically. It may be, for example, that Islamic laws of *shahādah* (testimony) could (and often do) provide an excellent approach to protecting the rights of the accused. When the classical formulations are examined in this perspective, it is not self-evident that the jury system combined with the admissibility of "circumstantial evidence" is intrinsically a better system for protecting the rights of the accused. But these important questions have, to my knowledge, hardly been discussed and especially not in dialogue.

Once a judicial procedure for such intercommunal cases was in place, various rules could govern the application of various laws. One possibility might be to apply the law of the party who won the case. This would obviously be simpler than trying to develop a completely new form of intercommunal law. Similar rules could govern the application of law in cases which do not involve two or more litigants. On the other hand, it may well turn out that developing a specifically intercommunal form of law (in line, perhaps, with an evolving international law) is the more equitable approach to such problems. I am not advocating any specifics here, only insisting that in the contemporary world we can no longer afford the luxury of developing our communal identities and institutions in conflict with each other rather than in dialogue with each other.

Many problems arise in connection with *ijtihād*, among them the change from the *ijmāʻ* (consensus) of the *'ulamā'* to government-sponsored deliberations and the tremendous amount of material needed for a new *ijtihād*. Even dialogue about this is riddled with problems. Many Muslims would be understandably ill at ease with even the thought of a non-Muslim thinking "creatively" about the *Sharīʻah*. It must be clearly understood that there is no possibility of a non-Muslim taking part in the process of *ijtihād*. Nevertheless, where there is a willingness (as there is in some quarters) to relate to non-Muslims as *Ahl al-Ṣulḥ* (in a treaty relationship) rather than as *Ahl al-Dhimmah* (protected subjects[9]), then there is room for this kind of discussion, both in theory and practice.

Even where there is an openness for dialogue, many problems remain in connection with *maqāṣid al-sharīʻah* (goals or purpose of the *Sharīʻah*) and the importance of the Qur'ān and Sunnah as *uṣul al-fiqh* (the primary sources of legal codification). Sūrat al-Tawbah (9:29) institutes *jizyah* — a tax to be paid by *dhimmi* communities under an Islamic government — and says it should be collected "with humiliation" — *wa hum ṣāghirūn*. In Bukhari we find a *Ḥadīth* to the effect that "Islam rules and is not ruled". The imams of the law schools quote a *Ḥadīth* that "no believer should be put to death because of a *kāfir*" and derive from it the ruling that *qiṣāṣ* (retaliation) does not apply to a Muslim who kills a non-Muslim. Ibn Taymiyyah quotes 'Umar Ibn al Khaṭṭāb as saying of the *dhimmiyīn*: "Humiliate them but do them no injustice"; and this becomes for him almost one of the *maqāṣid al-sharī'ah*, at least in relation to non-Muslims.[10]

These examples are not absolutes, but they do derive from Qur'ān and Sunnah and have functioned as important *shar'ī* (not just *fiqh*) principles. Of course, there have always been ways around them. Abū Ḥanifah, dissenting on the question of *qiṣāṣ* from the other founders of the classical *Madhāhib*, quotes both *Ḥadīth* and Qur'ān to support his opinion. He uses the *Ḥadīth*, "A believer who kills a *dhimmi* will not smell the odour of paradise, and yet it may be smelt at a distance of 40 years journey," and says the Qur'ān verse authorizing *qiṣāṣ* clearly makes no distinction between Muslim and non-Muslim (Sūrat al-Baqarah; 2:178). He then argues that *kāfir* in the other *Ḥadīth* refers to *ḥarbīs* (non-Muslim subjects of countries with whom the Muslim government has no treaty), not *dhimmiyīn*. His disciple Abu Yusuf specifically ruled that *dhimmiyīn* should *not* be humiliated when the *jizya* is collected.

Even so, the Qur'ān and *Ḥadīth* materials in question here are by any definition *shar'ī* principles and not just *fiqh*. They will need to be taken seriously in any formulation of Islamic law. Of course, they must be understood in the light of the whole Qur'ān and the full practice of the Prophet. Perhaps when the Qur'ān says God created different communities to vie with each other in justice (Sūrat al-Mā'idah; 5:51), the implication is that this is the sense in which Islam should rule and not be ruled: it should always win in the contest for justice.

Here we are in the realm of interpretation, and Abū Ḥanifah has shown in a very positive way the considerable scope in the ways in which the *Sharī'ah* is understood and applied. That brings us back to a practical problem: who is going to interpret the *Sharī'ah* and to what end? There is no system of law which cannot be subverted by those who administer it.

I am not speaking here only or even primarily about the deliberate, malicious perversion of justice in one's own personal interest. I am speaking about the values, goals and ideals shaped by history and by economic, sociological and psychological factors. Many people have spoken about Islam being used as a medium of self-expression and self-assertion. What happens when that self-expression is over against another, consciously or not, and when this adversarial self-expression is compounded by more than a little righteous anger at having been robbed and exploited, culturally, intellectually and materially, first by colonialism and then by economic imperialism?

To take these historical and psychological dimensions seriously is not necessarily to question the sincerity of faith to be found in the Islamist and other Islamic movements. Quite the contrary, I believe the faith is sincere and genuine and a cause for great hope. It does, however, raise serious questions about attempts at *ijtihād* which bypass the received tradition and seek to return to the "pure" Qur'ān and Sunnah — an approach typical of a number of groups and schools of thought generally referred to as "Salafiyyah". The following quotation from Sayyid Qutb, an influential thinker of the Muslim Brotherhood, is typical of this approach.

> The Islamic Law (*Sharī'ah*) is the work of God. Its source lies in the Qur'ān and the Sunnah. *Fiqh* (Islamic jurisprudence) is the work of men. They have elaborated it according to their own way of understanding, commenting on and applying the *Sharī'ah*, in particular circumstances, to answer particular needs, in the concrete conditions of the generation in which they lived, according to its way of understanding things, in appreciation of its goals and objectives, according to the interests dictated to them by the facts and circumstances... We must always remember that their judicial decision answered the concrete needs of their time. Even the theoretical prescriptions which they formulated and which they obeyed were inspired only by these needs, or better by the logic of the environment which surrounded them, by the age in which they lived, by the social ties and relations which prevailed in their milieu at that time.[11]

Some have criticized such views as reflecting an almost naive perception of a mythical "golden age". My own scepticism about them is based rather on the fact that such an unbridled "Salafiyyah" *ijtihād* is bound to reflect primarily the attitudes, values, concerns and experiences of those who do it. What Sayyid Qutb says of earlier attempts to codify the *Sharī'ah* applies equally to those who set about to do *ijtihād* today. The received tradition has many more and different influences at work within it, and this can be liberating. Of course, a selective reading of history cannot be avoided. But I would like to see much more emphasis placed on the value and richness of the classical tradition.

This is important precisely because I accept the basic sincerity of faith on the part of many participants in modern Islamic movements. They are sincere in their desire to serve God and committed to the search for justice in accordance with God's righteous will. If the whole tradition is valued — very definitely and emphatically — the liberating principles within it are also available to dialogue with perceptions formed from contemporary experience. It is clear, I hope, that I am not arguing for the implementation of classical *fiqh*. I believe there is no hope for justice in today's world apart from a new *ijtihād*. But I would like to see classical *fiqh* take a prominent, even central, place in the discussion concerning its development.

It might be argued that a new relationship, more open, positive and accommodating to non-Muslims, would develop in time even from a more Salafiyyah approach to *Sharī'ah* and *fiqh*. I have no doubt that it would, but I fear that the process would be painful and costly, both in terms of precious resources which need to be applied to pressing issues like poverty and education and at the cost of much human suffering and loss of life.

I think dialogue with Muslims about *Sharī'ah* is crucial. But I am not a Muslim; and while I do expect Muslims to listen to my concerns, I am aware as a committed religious believer that the first concern must be to listen to the Word of God. While some Muslims might listen seriously to my attempts to understand the Qur'ān and the Sunnah, I do not expect it. The body of classical *fiqh* enables me to express myself in Muslim terms and gives a much greater scope for discussion. I am not left alone with the believer and his or her best personal attempt to understand the Word of God. The same argument applies to homogeneous groups and their understanding of Qur'ān and Sunnah as to individuals. It is the breadth and variety of the classical tradition that is such a positive contribution to a new *ijtihād* in our modern context.

NOTES

1 Cf. the classic Arabic dictionary *Lisān al 'Arab* or Lane's *Arabic-English Lexicon*. Lane cites a number of classical sources on the etymology of the word and its particular semantic reference to a source of water.

2 The most sustained exposition of this view probably remains S.A. Rahman, *Punishment of Apostasy in Islam,* Lahore, Institute of Islamic Culture, 1972.

3 Antoine Fattal, *Le statut légal des non-musulmans en pays d'Islam*, Beirut, Imprimerie catholique, 1958, p.355.

4 Ibn Isḥāq, *Sīrat Rasūl Allah*, ed. Wüstenfeld, Leiden, Brill, 1858, p.342.

5 A.H. Al-Abdin, "The Sudan Charter", *Bulletin on Islam and Christian-Muslim Relations in Africa*, Vol. 6, no. 1, 1988, pp.1-12.

6 Cf. Amnon Cohen, *The Jews of Jerusalem*, Princeton, Princeton UP, 1984.

7 A.H. Al-Abdin, *op. cit.*, p.5.

8 *Ibid.*, p.6.

9 The word "subject" is more appropriate in this context. It is anachronistic to call *dhimmi* status "second-class citizenship". In the mediaeval world in which the law was formulated, there was no modern concept of "citizenship" but rather the concept of "subjects" of the appropriate government.

10 Ibn Taymiyyah, *Majmū'at al-Rasā'il wa al-Masā'il*, Beirut, 1913, esp. the section on "The Conditions of 'Umar concerning the Ahl al-Dhimmah".

11 Sayyid Qutb, *Naḥwa Mujtama' Islāmī*, Beirut, 6th ed., 1983, p.50.

9. Islamic *Sharī'ah* and the Status of Non-Muslims

GHAZI SALAHUDDIN ATABANI

In Islam, man *per se* is an object of exaltation. In narrating the story of creation, the Qur'ān extols the inherent merits of Adam, showing how he was honoured and favoured over other creatures. It also reveals that the earth and the rest of God's creation have been placed in subservience to man, in order for him to fulfil the purpose of his creation — the worship of God.

No human attribute deserves an eternal punishment or justifies enslavement and persecution by fellow human beings. Rather, the distinction among humans by colour of skin or language is merely intended for identification. The equality of human beings draws upon the commonality of their ancestral origin from the same male and female first to exist on earth.

God Almighty has honoured man most remarkably by bestowing him with a free conscience by which he can choose his faith. The Qur'ān states in absolute and final terms that "there shall be no compulsion in religion". People are free to have or not to have faith in God. The true reckoning is deferred to the hereafter where one will be punished or rewarded according to his belief and deeds.

While asserting the Islamic faith as the "true religion", Islam nevertheless leaves wide room for its followers to co-exist and intermingle with the followers of other faiths. The classification into Muslims and non-Muslims entails distinction in the hereafter, before God Almighty. It does not necessarily entail distinction or relegation in worldly terms. Moreover, this classification is based on a convertible criterion; in other words, the barriers it erects are surmountable. When Islam is compared with other civilizations which employed in their foundation the inconvertible criterion, or for that matter, the insurmountable barrier of ethnicity, it is evident, as Arnold Toynbee notes in *A Study of History*, how Islam acquired a formidable power of propagation within 20 years after the death of Prophet Muḥammad (PBUH).

In order to propagate the Islamic call, it was necessary to present Islam as a distinctive religion capable of liberation in this world and of salvation in the hereafter. Inevitably that necessitated a model (in this case the Muslim community) in which the ideals of Islam were exemplified and offered to the other communities around it. Thus, many religions preserved their vitality and even flourished within the world of Islam from the advent of the first Islamic state in Al Madīnah and passing through the different Islamic communities from the furthermost borders in Spain in the West and India in the East.

To elaborate this subject further, it will be useful to consider its theoretical framework derived from Islamic jurisprudence.

The theoretical framework

The Qur'ān is full of verses that call on Muslims to treat the People of the Scripture well. In so doing it invokes the common Abrahamic origins of Islam, Christianity and Judaism and calls for the observance by all of the common tenets of the three religions. Rather than indulging in sterile polemics with Christians and Jews, Muslims are encouraged to join hands with them in spreading monotheism, adhering to virtues and abstaining from vices.

The Qur'ān further elaborates that it is not forbidden to Muslims to show compassion and friendliness towards those who did not launch war against them or drive them out of their homes. Obviously, a friendly relationship with others is based on their attitude towards the existence of Islam and the freedom of its message, not on religion.

In order to encourage further the association with the People of the Scriptures, Muslims are permitted to marry from among them and to share meals with them. The significance of this can be seen against the background of the traditions of the Jews, who were contemporaries of the Muslims of Al Madīnah, since the former did not intermarry or share meals with the Muslims or the pagans of Arabia.

Though the People of the Scriptures enjoy a special status in Islam, Islamic teachings extend humane co-existence even to pagans. For example, a Muslim is required to maintain cordial relations with his kith and kin, but most importantly with his parents, even if they are idolaters. Also, Muslims in general are expected to sympathize with their brothers in humanity and extend a helping hand to them when calamities befall, regardless of their faith. The Prophet sent compassion money to the pagans of Makkah during a spell of drought, a gesture that looks very similar to humanitarian relief efforts of today. The Qur'ān goes even further to establish a gracious and unprecedented humanitarian principle by instructing its followers to grant asylum to those seeking it even if they are idolaters. All these teachings which advocate clemency, compassion and mercy, especially during a time of calamity or tribulation, underscore the importance Islam gives to purely human bonds.

When Muslims conquered new territories they left the peoples they met with the option of embracing Islam or remaining in their original faiths. Most opted for Islam, not due to coercion, but because they found in Islam a new liberating force. Islam represented social, political or even personal liberation to those who in earlier secular civilizations had been under the yoke of servitude and exploitation. Those who remained with their original beliefs acquired a special status and were called *dhimmiyīn*. Most of those were Christians, Jews or *majūs*. Those writers who have used the question of the *dhimmah* in order to level criticism at Islam have committed two oversights: first, by taking the concept of *dhimmah* out of its practical and historical context; second, by failing to realize that this status conferred a particularity on those non-Muslim communities which they desperately needed for their existence and without which they would have disappeared, willy-nilly.

Dhimmah literally means a contract concluded between Muslims and a certain group of non-Muslims who co-exist in one community. It is an everlasting contract which can be repealed by the non-Muslims, but not by Muslims. According to this contract, a non-Muslim enjoys all the rights and privileges the particular society offers except for holding a few posts that have a religious nature, for example, the head of state and the chief of the army. In return, the non-Muslim group pays a poll tax against each able-bodied adult male (females, children, old men and handicapped persons who cannot earn their living are exempted). It is important to note also that the non-Muslims do not pay the alm tax paid by the Muslims. Furthermore, if the non-Muslims engage in defending the community alongside their Muslim fellow citizens, the poll tax is automatically annulled.

To portray the exact nature of the *dhimmah* contract and to reveal how much protection was conferred by it, the statements of the Prophet (PBUH), the orthodox caliphs and the succeeding Muslim jurists must be carefully studied. Such study contradicts the claim that the *dhimmah* contract is intended to humiliate non-Muslims. The Prophet (PBUH) aligns himself with the *dhimmiyīn* by stating that "whoever harasses a *dhimmi* I shall be his adversary, and of whomever I become the adversary, I shall prosecute him in the Doomsday". 'Alī, the fourth orthodox caliph, declares: "He who has our *dhimmah* (contract), his blood is like our blood and his religion is like our religion." Hence the subsequent Muslim jurists stipulated an all-embracing legal principle in connection with the *dhimmiyīn* to the effect that "they are entitled to what we are entitled to and duty-bound to what we are duty-bound".

On this basis the jurists elaborate the rights of the *dhimmiyīn* in terms of protection from external aggression as well as internal oppression. In the former case, a *dhimmi* enjoys the same degree of protection provided to any Muslim. A *dhimmi* taken captive by the enemy is redeemed in the same way as a Muslim, by paying full ransom money. In the latter case, a *dhimmi* is even advantaged compared to a Muslim, for a Muslim may not be compensated for his money if it was earned illegally, for example by selling wine or pork, whereas a *dhimmi* must be compensated in such instance because those activities are not prohibited by his or her religion. Finally, a *dhimmi* is entitled not only to the annulment of the poll tax at old age, but also, like a Muslim, to the provident fund obtained from the state's *Bayt al-Māl* or treasury.

A quick comparison between the rights of the *dhimmi* in earlier Muslim communities and those stipulated in the Universal Declaration of Human Rights will show the extent to which the two correspond, despite the historical and cultural gap between them. The following are brief descriptions of the rights of non-Muslims under Islamic jurisprudence, in the four major categories of human rights. Straightforward rights like the right to life or to marriage have been omitted and emphasis placed on the more controversial aspects.

Civil rights. A *dhimmi* has the right to equality before the law, prosecution, appeal, the sanctity of his family and himself, freedom of conscience and choice of faith, freedom of worship and all the relevant religious expressions and celebrations, freedom to build temples and churches, freedom to express religious views and to argue with Muslims about their beliefs. Since "there shall be no compulsion in religion", a *dhimmi* woman may not be obliged to embrace Islam if she is married to a Muslim husband. *Dhimmiyīn* may be judged according to Muslim personal laws if they so wish, or according to their own personal laws. Differences in matters relating to marriage and divorce are well catered for.

Economic rights. Islam guarantees to *dhimmiyīn* the rights of work, of trade and of possessing and inheriting land and estate. In brief, they enjoy all economic rights on an equal footing with Muslims. A *dhimmi* is exempted from taxes of a religious nature such as *zakāt*.

Cultural rights. A *dhimmi* has the right to express his own culture, preserve his language and bring up his family in the manner he chooses.

Political rights. The early Muslim jurists attributed to *dhimmiyīn* all the political rights granted at that time to Muslims, including the assumption of high political and ministerial posts with the exception of certain posts which, because of their religious importance, required special qualifications which could not be met even by the majority of Muslims.

The historical experience

When the Holy Prophet of Islam (PBUH) established the first Islamic state at Al Madīnah he was driven by that spirit of tolerance provided for by the Qur'ān and enjoined by the Islamic faith. He opened up towards the Jews, who then represented the non-Muslim community of Al Madīnah. His positive approach was enhanced by an ecumenical aspiration which recognized the common origin of the messages of Moses and Muḥammad (PBUH). Accordingly, he concluded with the Jews of Al Madīnah the first constitutional document in Islam, known as the "Al Madīnah Document", intended to integrate the Jews into a united community with the Muslims. The document stipulated that the Jews were an integral part of the community of Al Madīnah alongside the followers of Islam, thus establishing the tenets of a united and harmonious society.

Unfortunately, when the Jews tried to enter into a new secret alliance with the pagans of Mecca, the Al Madīnah Document was abrogated and war between the two sides inevitably broke out. However, the Prophet's treatment of the Jews before the relationship turned sour was characterized by profound respect. Of the many interesting stories reported by historians in this connection, the best known and most telling is the sign of respect he showed at the funeral of a Jewish man by rising to his feet. When the Prophet's companions disapproved of this action, he reproached them, asking whether they did not consider the soul of a Jew to be a human soul. He was thus laying the foundations of a strong human brotherhood. Equally respectful was the Prophet's treatment of Christians from Najran in southern Arabia who visited him in Al Madīnah. When it was the time for their prayers, he left them alone in his own mosque so that they could have privacy.

The orthodox caliphs followed in the Prophet's footsteps in their treatment of Jews and Christians. When the second orthodox caliph 'Umar entered the Jerusalem church and the bishops offered him a chance to pray inside it, he refused simply because he feared that such an act might goad later Muslims to convert it into a mosque.

The protection that the Holy Prophet extended to the Christians of Yemen while he was in Al Madīnah went beyond the mere respect for their rites. He offered them covenants in which he bestowed on them his own protection. He further safeguarded their property and money, their person and land, and secured for them everything related to their faith. When Khālid Ibn al-Walīd conquered Bahrain he did likewise for the Christians there. 'Umar the second orthodox caliph approved of this.

An examination of the status of the People of the Scriptures and others, including the Magians, under various Islamic governments, whether in India, Baghdad, Egypt, Morocco or Spain, would show how much they prospered. Not only were their lives, property and creeds safeguarded, but they in fact held high public jobs, took ministerial posts or even worked as caliphs' advisors. This indicates the effective role they played in Muslim societies, for which they were qualified by virtue of their status as *dhimmiyīn*.

Contemporary implementation of *Sharī'ah*

The fortunes of non-Muslims vary from one Islamic country to another, although the predominant practice in the different Muslim societies is tolerance, the legacy of Islam's high moral ground that governs most Islamic societies.

An experience that deserves serious study in the contemporary context is that of Sudan, for it brings together important characteristics which on the face of it appear conflicting and irreconcilable. Indeed, Sudan, which is currently applying laws derived from Islamic *Sharī'ah*, is a multi-religious, multi-cultural and multi-linguistic society.

In the Islamic experience of Sudan, the non-Muslim Sudanese is not regarded as a protected person or *dhimmi*. Rather the status of non-Muslims is compared to that of the Jews of Al Madīnah, who entered into a contractual relationship with the Muslims. This entails that they derive their rights by virtue of their citizenship within the framework of the constitution and the law. Such relationship is based on the historical fact that in a modern state, whether in Sudan or elsewhere, the non-Muslims have not acquired their status following a war with the Muslims as did the *dhimmiyīn*. Rather, their status is that of natural citizens, an important attribute that determines the treatment of non-Muslims in modern Islamic societies on perfectly equal footing with Muslims.

The status of non-Muslims in Sudan today may be summed up in five salient features:

1. Equality in rights and duties irrespective of race, culture, creed or ethnic origin, including political rights such as holding of public posts, nomination and election.

2. Custom and *Sharīʻah* as the two sources of legislation. The custom and tradition of non-Muslims have thus become an important tributary of national legislation, which enables them to preserve their specific character and identity.

3. Adoption of legal pluralism at two levels: (a) the federal level, so that states having a non-Muslim majority are exempted from the application of *ḥudūd* and other penalties of specific religious nature; (b) the personal level, within the states that apply Islamic laws, so that non-Muslims are not subject to legal pursuit for actions which their religious denomination does not consider to be crimes punishable by law, such as consumption of alcohol, fornication, defamation and apostasy. Non-Muslims are also exempted from taxes of Islamic nature, for example, *zakāt* or alm tax. They do not pay poll tax but pay other taxes which Muslims pay.

4. Full expression of the religious and cultural identities of non-Muslims, including the right to raise their families according to their faith and culture. Muslims are enjoined to show respect and protect them.

5. Commitment by non-Muslims to uphold the duties of citizenship and to respect the Islamic faith and the right of the Muslim majority to express itself fully in the form of its religion, including political expression.

This experience is charting a successful course despite obstacles placed in its way. Practical implementation of *Sharīʻah* in Sudan has enabled the clarification of two misperceptions: that *Sharīʻah* is monolithic and inflexible and that it picks on non-Muslims for penalty. In fact, the flexibility offered by legal pluralism is unparalleled anywhere, not even in the industrialized countries which claim full equality among their subjects. And we have already seen that Christians are not subject to specific penalties on a selective basis. On the contrary, whatever they do which is not considered to be an offence in their own religious denomination is not punishable under *Sharīʻah*.

Both in theory and as demonstrated by its historical application, Islamic *Sharīʻah* surpasses the declarations of human rights and the slogans of prominent revolutions, in that it bases the rights of non-Muslims on clear-cut divine provisions that the faithful must carry out. In fact these constitute part of a Muslim's daily prayers. *Sharīʻah* gives the rights of non-Muslims an added power and sanctity which constitutions and laws fall short of providing. Evidence of this are the current ethnic uprisings in many countries, which have further undermined the theoretical equality provided by many secular constitutions.

Part III

10. Muslim Minorities and *Sharīʿah* in Europe

GÉ SPEELMAN

Muslim minorities

A conservative estimate places the number of Muslims living in Western Europe at approximately 7.5 million: 2.5 million in France, 2 million in Germany, 1.5 million in the UK, 500,000 in the Netherlands, 250,000 in Belgium, 130,000 in Scandinavia, 100,000 in Austria and 500,000 in Italy. These numbers do not include refugees.[1]

For most of these communities, minority status as Muslims is quite a new experience. I say "minority status *as Muslims*", because the societies from which Pakistani, North African, Turkish and Sub-Saharan African communities in Europe come are of course far from homogeneous. Regional, linguistic and cultural differences were the most important markers of identity for these communities in their countries of origin. In Western Europe they are suddenly regarded as belonging to one group: Muslim migrants.

One effect which this has had is that people who belonged to religious minorities in their "homeland" breathe more freely and talk more openly of their religious affiliation. The Alevite Turkish community in the Netherlands, for instance, is experiencing a modest religious and cultural revival.

For mainstream Sunnī Muslims of the first generation, minority status can be quite threatening. They react by strongly reaffirming their religious and cultural background. This results in a rapid growth of mosque associations. In some communities regional cultural differences are perpetuated in these associations. An average first-generation Moroccan in the Netherlands still feels primarily that he is, for example, a Berber from the city of Nador and will associate with a mosque set up by other citizens of Nador. In a predominantly migrant neighbourhood in one Dutch city, the board of three church schools wanted to talk to the parents of their Muslim pupils and so decided to get in touch with the neighbourhood mosque. They discovered that in fact there were 17 different mosque associations in this neighbourhood. Mosque associations may also be divided along political lines. This is quite visible within the Turkish community in Germany, for example.

The net result of the first generation's struggle to preserve their Muslim and cultural identity is thus a great variety of Muslim organizations. The younger generation no longer has the vivid picture of life "back home" and everything it implies. They often struggle with their parents over cultural taboos and outdated educational concepts. But their experiences with native Europeans are no less frustrating. Between the Scylla of the parental home and the Charybdis of a hostile majority community, they try to define their identity.

For many youth, Islam is an important part of that identity, although this does not always translate into regular mosque attendance. A recent Dutch survey showed that about 10 percent of the youth of Turkish descent and 20 percent of the youth of Moroccan descent visit the mosque on a regular basis. Young people are often quite critical of the atmosphere in the mosque. I remember a conversation with two Turkish girls. One was extremely critical of the way the local *hoja* (religious teacher) had taught Islamic principles. She objected particularly to his old-fashioned teaching methods and authoritarian attitude. We came to talk about her forthcoming marriage and the children she hoped to have. When I asked, "What will you teach your children about religion?", she replied, "The most important thing they have to learn is that they are Muslims. They will not learn about all the old-fashioned things my parents taught me, like how a woman should behave towards her father-in-law; but they should learn what a Muslim must know and do." When I went on to ask the two of them how they hoped to see the religious education of their children attended to, they had quite a debate, but they ended up by saying with a sigh, "We are afraid they will have to go to the same old *hoja*. We have nobody else here."

From this and similar experiences I conclude that for some young Muslims born or reared in Europe, local customs which their parents saw as intimately tied to religion, such as rules of behaviour vis-à-vis parents-in-law, no longer have the same religious meaning. They look for an Islam that is different, that is "wholly religious" in content. This seems to be a logical development when Muslims of different cultural background are thrown together. But one should not underestimate the continuous importance of *'urf* or *'adāt*, the local customs parents take from their homeland, for even the next generation. Local ideas about Islam will continue to stand in the way of unity among European Muslims for quite some time yet.

The European host community

In 1991 there was an extended political debate in the Netherlands about the integration of migrants. Although the neutral term "migrants" was used, almost all the concrete issues mentioned in the debate were about Muslim migrants. A central question was that of the "limits of tolerance" in a liberal society confronted with radically different cultural concepts about, for instance, equality between women and men.

Although the debate was along predictable lines, with unfounded stereotypes of the Muslim community heard repeatedly, its implications are interesting. For twenty years various European societies have maintained the concept of "multiculturalism" with respect to migrant communities. The ideal of multiculturalism was put into words by Roy Jenkins, in 1966. "Integration", he said, did not mean the loss by immigrants of their own national characteristics. "We do not need a melting pot, which will turn everyone out in a common mould... I define 'integration' not as 'assimilation' but as equal opportunity, coupled with cultural diversity, in an atmosphere of mutual tolerance." On the whole, our programme should be to build such a society. The freedom of ethnic minorities to live their own cultural life should be restricted only in a limited number of cases where it could threaten the well-being of the whole population.

In theory, we are moving towards such a society. In fact, there is little space for different cultural concepts in the existing European states. The subconscious ideal for many Europeans seems to be that of the monolithic nation-state, in which people who live in one territory (marked by state boundaries) speak one language, share one history and have one culture. That this concept is based on myths about the past rather than reality does not seem to prevent people of the majority culture from discriminating against people from the diverse minorities. In the specific debate about the acceptability of Muslims and their culture, certain prescripts of *Sharī'ah* play a role. For example, Ḥanafī punishments are sometimes cited by Europeans as proof that there is no place for Muslim culture in European nation-states.

Sharī'ah

Sharī'ah has always been a rallying cry for Muslims bent on preserving their faith. But we should not close our eyes to the fact that not every

Muslim lived according to the prescripts of *Sharīʻah* prior to his or her migration to Europe. On the one hand, most Muslim countries have codified law which is partly or wholly different from *Sharīʻah* precepts. Since 1926 Turkish citizens living in Europe have had a family law based on Swiss civil law. On the other hand, what many migrants consider "Islamic" or "according to *Sharīʻah*" often has very strong roots in local custom. In *Sharīʻah* law there has always been legitimate place for *ʻurf* or *ʻadāt*. For migrants, however, it can be very confusing to discover that "their" *Sharīʻah* is not the only possible one, a fact pressed home by their confrontation with Muslims from other cultural backgrounds.

Sharīʻah is about the whole of Muslim life and Muslim society. Most Muslims, however, do not attempt to transplant an Islamic society into the European context. With the exception of some Muslims in Britain, *Sharīʻah* has been defined as a local community system, not as something which might affect the surrounding society. As far as Muslims in Europe are concerned, the most important areas under debate here are those dealing with the *ʻibādāt* (forms of worship) in the broadest sense and with family law.

Regarding the *ʻibādāt*, a point of primary concern for first-generation Muslim migrants is the basic question of how to pass them on to the next generation. Most parents are confronted with children who want to know not only *how* to pray, fast and the like, but also *why* it is necessary to do so. In present-day European experience religion is not self-evident. This does not necessarily mean that religion has disappeared from the scene, but it does mean that no specific form of religion is the cultural norm. Religion has become individualized: the individual has become the autonomous authority for belief. Young Muslims will time and again be confronted with the question: "Why do *you* believe (or do) this?" When they pass this question on to their parents, the latter do not feel equipped to answer it. A major factor contributing to the foundation of mosques (which in turn serve as a basis for Islamic education) is the powerlessness of parents when their children ask them about *ʻibādāt*.

Imāms can play a very important role, not only in the passing on of *Sharīʻah* but also as community leaders. However, they are often hindered by their lack of experience with European secular society and the extensive demands the community makes on them. In the Netherlands, groups of Imāms from both the Moroccan and Turkish communities have been following short courses to learn something about Dutch society, history, politics and churches. Even so, most do not speak Dutch. A small working group is trying to set up plans for imām-training at Amsterdam

University. I think it would help very much if at least some imāms were born and reared in the European context.

Following certain precepts also creates problems. In general those precepts which have strictly personal, individual consequences are rarely problematic. The precepts of the *'ibādāt* that touch on public life, however, arouse resistance in society as a whole and from local authorities in particular. It is quite possible to pray at home, of course. But when Muslims want to build a mosque, they often meet with neighbourhood resistance, and if they want to call the *'adhān* from the mosque five times a day, they will almost certainly run counter to public authorities. *Ḥalāl* slaughter is not possible everywhere, even after years of struggle. Burials according to Muslim rites were permitted in the Netherlands only after changes in the law. Not every Muslim can get days off for the major festivals.

But even practices which do not touch public order and seem purely personal may create an outrage. A clear example is the French head-scarves affair of 1989. To understand why French authorities were so adamant about prohibiting Muslim schoolgirls from wearing the scarves, it is necessary to recognize the extreme forms of laicism that have been part of French history since the French revolution (it is no coincidence that this affair took place in the year of the bicentenary of the revolution). Yet it is clear that the prohibition had some anti-Islamic, even racist overtones.

A field in which *Sharī'ah* is highly debated both among European Muslims and between Muslims and native Europeans is the law of marriage and divorce. It should be noted that there are great differences here among European countries and among the different Muslim countries of origin. Whereas Turkish family law has hardly any formal link with *Sharī'ah*, the Moroccan *mudawwanah* is mainly based on Malikī jurisdiction. In some cases, the difference between legal systems can create tensions within Muslim families.

It can be both offensive and problematic for a Muslim father to discover that his children by a second wife are not considered his legal offspring. Women living in Europe will often appeal to European judges for a "European" alimony in case of *ṭalāq*-divorce. A European judge can spare the woman the long and often troublesome procedure of *taṭlīq* or divorce, but the decision of a European judge may not be recognized in the home country, which causes new difficulties for the parties involved. In one case, a Moroccan woman obtained a divorce in a Dutch court. Her ex-husband did not recognize the divorce and made an appeal to a

Moroccan court when his ex-wife visited Morocco with her new spouse. In the eyes of the Moroccan judge her second marriage was considered illegal, and the woman and her second husband were imprisoned for adultery.

Some groups of Muslims in Britain have organized action for the recognition by English courts of *Sharī'ah* law of marriage and divorce. They have met with resistance in the British Parliament. At a conference on this subject, the following objections were brought forward by a British lawyer:

— There are different Muslim schools of law. Many Muslim countries have formulated their own family law code. What particular Muslim family law should be applied?

— Would cases be decided by a civil court or by a special *Sharī'ah* court? If the first, how can an English judge correctly interpret *Sharī'ah* law? If the second, could the different groups of Muslims in Britain agree about the interpretation of *Sharī'ah*?

— The most fundamental objection: to Western minds some points of Muslim family law seem to violate some human rights as laid down in international conventions, especially rights guaranteeing equality of men and women in marriage. Muslims will argue that their call for *Sharī'ah* law is based on another human right, the right of the freedom of religion. But freedom of religion is subject to limitations if these are necessary to protect public safety, health, order or morals or the fundamental rights and freedoms of others. One of these fundamental rights is the right to sexual equality. In three instances, Muslim family law is, in my opinion, clearly discriminating against women:

• The prohibition of Muslim women marrying non-Muslim men, while Muslim men may marry Christian or Jewish women.

• Polygamy, as it allows one spouse to take further partners while denying such a right to the other spouse, is discriminatory. The Muslim argument that Westerners take mistresses does not really counter this: it confuses law with practice. Besides, the Western practice is not discriminatory. Wives, too, can have a lover.

• *Ṭalāq*-divorce also clearly seems discriminatory. Again, the arguments that wives can stipulate their right to initiate a *ṭalāq*-divorce in their marriage contract, and that a *ṭalāq*-divorce can cost the husband a lot of money, are confusing the law with practice.

The opinions expressed here are representative of European reactions to Muslim proposals for their own rules of *alaḥwāl al shakhṣiyyah*. These three areas are in fact the greatest sources of tension between the different European systems of family law and those of many Muslim communities.

To my knowledge no Muslim has ever expressed an urgent wish to see *ḥadd* punishment administered in the sphere of penal law, although that seems to be the major concern of native Europeans when they talk about *Sharī'ah* law.

Towards multiculturalism

If Europeans really want to live in multicultural societies, a great number of steps remain to be taken. Equal opportunity, emancipation of minority groups, anti-racist education are all necessary but not sufficient conditions. As to *Sharī'ah* law, the majority will have to change its attitude to the public manifestations of Islam. This is in fact a marginal adjustment compared to the kinds of change that minorities are obliged to undergo, but it would make a substantial difference to Muslims if, for example, local authorities would not panic when Muslims asked for the broadcasting of the *'adhān* but would try to work out a plan (together with the mosque committee) for informing the neighbourhood, or if school authorities would not be squeamish about Muslim dress. For this to happen, it seems important that the majority let go of the myths of the monocultural origin of the nation-state.

The majority should also seriously consider the possibility of setting up law courts to which Muslims could go to settle their family affairs in the Muslim way. There are some serious problems in this domain, however. One is this: if faced with the personal choice between, say, having an Islamic *talāq* or a European divorce, I fear that many Muslim women in Europe would opt for the latter. So far, the Muslim community has done little to persuade women that *Sharī'ah* ultimately gives them the best deal. This is certainly a point to be discussed. It also raises the question of whose choice prevails — that of the individual or that of the community? To European thinking, the individual inevitably takes precedence.

As far as the minority is concerned, it would help if able religious leaders, capable of real *ijtihād*, would help the Muslim communities to find ways to apply *Sharī'ah* in a different context. I am aware that in many countries of origin, new ways are being explored to institute divorce. Muslims in Europe are not always up-to-date on these developments. Although polygamy does not seem to be a major problem for Muslim women in Europe, for some it does constitute a nuisance. Here, too, better education of both men and women might help. Another issue that needs addressing is that of mixed marriages in which the wife is the Muslim partner. Such marriages do occur, and the Muslim community has no ready answer to them.

Most important of all, a debate is needed on the precise nature of *Sharī'ah*. The following remarks, cited from a discussion between English Protestants and Muslims, point to some of the issues:

> There seems to be a difference between the Western [Protestant] Christian concept of law and *Sharī'ah*. English common law is regarded as a purely human creation. Law reflects the moral values of a particular culture, a particular phase in history. It is susceptible to change. Protestant Christians regard the law as a reflection of the human failure to live directly under God. In their view, the relation between God and humankind, between one human being and another, are central. Relations are dynamic. Law only serves and regulates those relations.
>
> But does the fact that *Sharī'ah* in Islam is of divine origin mean that it must be static? One can distinguish in Islam between *Dīn* (faith) and *Sharī'ah* (belief). *Sharī'ah* is an expression of *Dīn* (note: Christian theologians would distinguish between *fides qua* = *Dīn*, faith as an attitude, and *fides quae* = *Sharī'ah*, the content of faith, what must be believed). Every prophet (Nuh, Ibrahim) had his own *shar'*, according to the Muslim theologian Qurtubī. That is why we distinguish four sources for *Sharī'ah*: Qur'ān, Sunnah, *ijmā'* and *ijtihād*. The Qur'ān is the ultimate source. But the Qur'ān needs to be interpreted. Therefore *Sharī'ah* is in fact a very dynamic whole.

NOTE

1 Much of the information in this paper comes from a long-term study project organized by the Churches' Committee for Migrants in Europe (CCME) called Muslim Minorities and *Sharī'ah* in Europe. Muslims and Christians in a dozen Western European countries have gathered material and compared notes for it.

Part IV

11. Secularism and Religion

MOHAMMED BEN-YUNUSA

The concept of secularism has many dimensions and is perceived from different angles by different people. It has implications for politics, religion, economics, society, education and culture.

At one level, secularism connotes the dissociation of certain aspects of life from others. It sets a dividing line between two or more disciplines with the ultimate aim of allowing each to perform its function effectively. Some sociologists would argue that secularism aims to establish a functional relationship between different sectors of society. It is imperative to note that secularism and secular societies do allow for new and different ideas to come in and thus facilitate contact with other societies and their value systems.

Secularism in the mediaeval period connoted the tendency for religious persons to dispense with human affairs and to meditate on God and the afterlife. At the time of the Renaissance it took a different direction and manifested itself in the development of humanism. This was the period when Muslims began to show more interest in human cultural achievements.

Within the European church the concept of secularism is often viewed as anti-religious, because the movement towards secularism in the 20th-century West suggested that religion — in particular, Christianity — should limit its concern to God and the sacred duties of life. However, at the same time a number of theologians were beginning to advocate that not only should Christianity be concerned with God and sacred duties, but also that people should find in the secular world an opportunity to participate in everyday life in a way that would promote Christian values, thereby discovering the real meaning of the message of Christ.

Some thinkers have portrayed secularism as an ethical system founded on the principles of natural morality and independent of revealed religions. On this view, the basis of secularism is freedom of thought, the right of every person to think for himself. Implied in this is the right to hold a different opinion on any subject. Thus any vital custom is open to debate.

In politics, secularism argues for a government that is independent of any religious function or organization, meaning that no religion is recognized or adopted as a state religion. In essence, European-Christian thinkers believed this approach would enable individuals to participate actively in running the affairs of state without having their religious inclinations distract them from serving their nation and discharging their duty to develop it, though they would be free to practise their religion after office hours.

In the social sphere, secularism denies that religion has any bearing on the source of our legal system. Hence corruption, nepotism, sectionalism, tribalism are encouraged within the system. The concept of secularism is also conspicuous within the realm of education. It attempts to produce a type of education that has no relation at all to a religious outlook, on the ground that mixing secular subjects with religion might create a conflict of ideas on certain fundamental issues. This was especially evident when Aristotelian physics became the established way of knowing the world, and Occidental man was cut off from transcendental reality. This has been described as a "metaphysical catastrophe". Objectivity became the yardstick in the scientific world: what cannot be seen visibly does not exist. The teaching of such doctrines as God, soul, life after death, paradise and hell were seen as obsolete and became extinct.

Religiously, the concept of secularism may also be seen as the Christian doctrine of the separation of the state from religion, pure and simple. The concept is said to have emanated from the biblical expression, "Render unto Caesar the things which are Caesar's and unto God the things which are God's. My kingship is not of this world". These words of Jesus imply that there are certain things reserved for human beings and others meant for God; and this marks the beginning of secularism as the separation of state from religion.

In sum, the concept of secularism may have the following denotations:

1. A movement in society directed away from other-worldliness to this-worldliness.
2. The development of interest in human cultural achievement and in the possibilities of human fulfilment in this world.

3. Freedom of thought: each person has the right to think for himself and to differ in opinion on any subject.
4. Enabling an individual to see good for himself.
5. "Render to Caesar what is Caesar's and to God what is God's."
6. A definite professed system of belief denoting a mode of thought more or less implicitly held and acted upon.

The concept of religion

Throughout history religion has been misunderstood and abused. Some people use it as a means of exploitation and suppression, a pretext for prejudice and persecution. Others use it as a source of power and domination. In the name of religion, unjustifiable wars have been launched, freedom of thought and conscience suppressed, science persecuted, the right of the individual to maturity denied, human dignity and honour flagrantly debased. The injustices inflicted on humanity in the name of religion have meant that religion itself has suffered many losses.

These are historical facts which no one can deny. But is this the proper function of religion or the right approach to it? Could this be the purpose of religion? The indisputable answer is an emphatic No. There are many religions in the world, and each claims to be the one and only true religion. Each religion is supposed to have come from God for the right guidance of humanity. But these claims contradict each other, causing dissension among people and vehement reactions to religion, instead of welding humanity into one universal brotherhood under the one universal benevolent God. This situation makes any neutral observer at least confused if not averse to any kind of religion.

The Islamic concept of religion is unique. It is true that genuine religion must come from God for the right guidance of humankind. It is equally true that human nature and major human needs are basically the same at all times. This leads to one conclusion: there is one true religion coming from the one and the same God to deal with the outstanding human problems of all times.

This religion is Islam. But it should be borne in mind that Islam was not taught by the Prophet Muḥammad alone. On the contrary, Islam had been taught by the all the prophets before Muḥammad; and the true followers of Abraham and Moses as well as those of Jesus and the rest were all called Muslims. So Islam has been and will continue to be the true universal religion of God, because God is one and changeless and because human nature and major human needs are fundamentally the same, irrespective of time and place, of race and age, and of any other consideration.

With this in mind, Islam maintains that religion is not only a spiritual and intellectual necessity but also a social and universal need. It is not meant to bewilder us but to guide us. It is not designed to debase us but to elevate our moral nature. Its aim is not to deprive us of anything useful or to burden or oppress us, but to open for us inexhaustible treasures of sound thinking and right action. It is not to confine us narrowly but to launch us into wide horizons of truth and goodness. In short, true religion is to acquaint us with God as well as with ourselves and the rest of the universe.

True religion satisfies human spiritual and moderate material needs. It unties one's psychological knots and complexes, sublimates one's instincts and aspirations and disciplines one's desires and the whole course of life. It improves one's knowledge of God — the highest truth in the universe — and of one's own self. It teaches one about the secrets of life and human nature, about good and evil, about right and wrong. It purifies the soul from evil, clears the mind from doubts, strengthens the character and corrects the thinking and convictions.

All this can be achieved only when one faithfully observes the spiritual duties and physical regulations introduced by religion. On the other hand, true religion educates and trains a person in hope and patience, in truthfulness and honesty, in love for the right and good, in courage and endurance — all of which are required for mastery of the great art of living. Moreover, true religion ensures against fears and spiritual losses and assures one of God's aid and unbreakable alliance. It provides peace and security and makes life meaningful.

That is what true religion can do for humanity, and that is the concept of religion in Islam. Any religion which fails to bear these fruits is not Islam, or rather is not religion, is not religious or God-minded. God is absolutely true when he says in the holy Qur'ān: "Verily the religion with God is Islam. Nor did the People of the Book dissent therefrom except through envy of each other, after knowledge had come to them. But if any deny the signs of God, God is swift in calling to account" (3:19). "And if anyone desire a religion other than Islam, never will it be accepted of him and in the hereafter he will be in the ranks of those who have lost [all spiritual good]" (3:85).

Secularism and religion

The main aim of secularism was to eliminate the dominance of religion in human affairs by providing a system according to which people would develop on a purely social and intellectual basis. The initial idea was to give people a chance to develop policies dictated by social exigencies, totally uninfluenced by religious biases and intimidation. But while theoretically embarking on the institution of an objective social system, it subsequently lost its early attitude of indifference to religion and apparent neutrality.

As we have intimated, secularism arose as a protest movement, and as such acquired the vehemence of all such movements and the driving passion that normally accompanies them. On the face of it, it presented a policy of non-involvement in religion. But this non-involvement can take two forms: total indifference to religion or active opposition to it. When the latter occurs, secularism becomes a "religion" of its own.

Marxism was a form of secularism that made no attempt to hide its opposition to religion. Nevertheless, even though Marxist philosophy looked upon religion as "the opiate of the people", Marxism itself was a philosophy of life, a blueprint for political and social harmony and thus in that sense a religious ideology. If the neutrality propagated by secularism thus turns out to be just as religious as the dogmas and doctrines it set out to neutralize, the question arises whether any country can be truly secular, that is, completely free of involvement in affairs of religion. With this question in mind, we take a look at secularism and secularity.

Secularity and secularism

We have shown how secularism attempted to construct a platform for human development based on a kind of moral independence from religious doctrines and worship. At first glance, it seems that such a system could operate alongside religious beliefs. But we have also seen that this ideal has not been realized, and secularism has often brought with it the same stringencies which it opposed in religion. In the final analysis one is forced to group secularism with other ideologies and doctrines that go under the heading "religion".

"Secularity", on the other hand, can more appropriately be seen as a state of being neutral in religious affairs, neither opposing nor promoting religion. Far from being totally uninterested in religion, it acknowledges the existence of religion and appreciates that members of the "secular community" are at the same time adherents of diverse religious beliefs. As such it respects those beliefs while at the same time keeping a watchful eye to see that religion does not overstep its bounds and infringe on matters of public interest, thereby jeopardizing public peace.

The supreme secular authority has the task of regulating the ever-evolving social life according to the dictates of an order unchangeable in its universal and moral principles. It must make it easier for persons to attain physical, intellectual and moral perfection in the temporal order and not impede their achievement of their spiritual and supernatural aspirations.

Religious bodies within a secular state expect the state to take an interest in both the temporal and spiritual welfare of its citizens. It can do this by maintaining the rule of order through the means put at its disposal by the community and by facilitating the citizens' practice of their religion.

In a multi-religious society, this will certainly be the safest course for the government to take. Indeed, history has shown that there has never been smooth sailing for governments that adopt theocracy or attempt to marry religion and politics. Such policies tend to camouflage political jealousies and dissatisfactions. Christianity as a state religion did not thrive for long even with the boost it got in the 4th and 8th centuries under Constantine and Charlemagne respectively. Today we witness the woes of Islamic fundamentalism in countries like Iran, Iraq, Lebanon and even Nigeria. In these cases political conflicts are being thrashed out under the canopy of religious revival and neo-puritanism.

In short, whenever a state becomes actively involved in religion, the consequences are unsavoury. And the problems are further compounded when there is a multiplicity of religions, since the government is exposed to the danger of partiality towards one of them, either because it is the majority religon or for political convenience. Thus a government that hopes to survive as a "secular" state must remember and uphold its true aim, which is to help individual persons to a healthy social growth without hampering their spiritual growth. That way the state guards against the violation of the inherent rights of human persons and can then justifiably demand that they in turn perform their civic duties.

For their part, religious bodies must not intervene unjustifiably in the government of the things of the world. Occasionally religious bodies (the church especially) deem it necessary and appropriate to champion the cause of freedom and fair-play against state absolutism. Such intervention has been considered by secularists and totalitarians as unjustifiable interference in the political arena. However, the fact remains that even if the church accepts indifference to religion and the state monopoly on purely human affairs, the church is at the service of humanity as such, that is, of persons in all their conditions, limitations and needs. In the face of state extremism it cannot fail to reassert its role as the custodian of moral and social ethics and the sentinel for political behaviour.

The challenges of secularism

There are no real contradictions between secularism in its positive ethical content and Islam in its secular content. However, differences between the two do exist in relation to their respective ideas about regulating human life in its totality and in their distinct concepts of the motives and ends of conduct. Islam makes legitimate secular claims whereas secularism does not advance any extra-secular pretensions.

From the Islamic point of view, religion is an organic whole, and the secular aspect of it is inseparable from the extra-secular aspect. Separating out the secular aspect is tantamount to accepting the message in part, which is in effect rejecting the whole. The secular cannot have a separate existence in an essentially Islamic civilization. Therefore, secularism in its Western connotation and current technical usage may be justifiably referred to in the Islamic context as de-Islamization.

Secularism is nevertheless a legitimate Western social theory. Like other modern Western ideologies, secularism is intentionally ethical and morally positive in conception. It is characterized by the same limited outlook and perception as other ideologies, necessitated by the fact that they evolved to cater for specific problems at a specific period of time in Western Europe. The history of secularism would indicate that the movement was a natural culmination of processes and problems that are essentially Western. It was a reaction against social wrongs and the moral philosophy of 19th-century Western European society. It was a protest movement against the selfishness and greed of the wealthy and influential classes and the solid dogma and theology of the Christian church. The continued resistance to reform and change and the resultant pressure of class conflict set in motion a movement to find an alternative moral philosophy and social system. A system was needed that would recognize the necessity of furthering social and political progress outside the established system, which had presumably failed. Morally and ethically secularism was positive. But because the established system was based on religious and supernatural presuppositions, secularism was necessarily religiously negative and at best indifferent.

The main criticism against secularism came from the Christian church. Secularism dissociated itself from Christian religious connections in its search for a moral philosophy and positive policy, relying instead on the independence of secular truth based on the experience of this life as maintained and tested by reason alone. Rejecting all Christian religious pretensions, it sought human improvement by material means alone. The nature of secularism and the extent to which it differed from the Christian religion are evident from its historical and philosophical antecedents. Secularism was influenced by social, political and philosophical theories that are actually anti-religious. It established its claim to furnish a theory of life and conduct by an appeal to philosophy and ethics. Its anti-theistic, positivist concept supplied the basis for the separation. Its antecedents in utilitarianism gave it its non-religious explanation of the motives and ends of conduct.

The secularist thesis is that human improvement and progress can be achieved by material means alone. Therefore only knowledge that is based on the experience of this life can be explained by reason and science. At the time of its inception, the relations between Christianity and rationalism and between Christianity and science were not good. The secularist saw the possibility of establishing a theory of life on the basis of rational knowledge and science without resort to religion. If it chose to speak on spiritual matters, it would have some divided claims, but by limiting its propositions, aspirations and interests to the material sphere, secularism was on safe ground within the general context of Western society.

Secularism can therefore only be seen as a Western solution to Western problems. It is the end result of historical situations and processes. The West has not been fortunate in its political and ideological history in that it lacks unitive polity and philosophy. Christianity, the leading Western ideology, has from its inception and in its development refused to attempt or failed to incorporate into its dogma those material aspects of life for which humans have shown more interest. The Christian ideals include the separation of state from religion, of secular from spiritual life, of theology from science. Because its prime objective is salvation of the soul, Christianity opts for the spirit, leaving the determinants of the spirit to the other organs of social organization.

Part IV

12. Religion and Secularization

Introductory Remarks from a Western-Christian Perspective

HEINZ KLAUTKE

The nature of secularization

Secularization is understood in very different ways. It was said in a recent congress on Europe and Islamic culture that Muslims cannot understand "secularized religiosity" in the West. In another conference it was stated that the pluralistic and secular way of thinking which is characteristic and symptomatic of Western culture is seen by Muslims as the "fall of man", as decay. Secularization is equated with rootless relativism.[1]

But there are differences of understanding not only between Muslims and Christians but also within these groups. On the one hand, the age of Enlightenment and the resulting secularization are seen as the source of all evil, immorality and perversion, especially in the Western world. Sometimes this seems to be a formula used by Muslims to describe the West in a negative way. On the other hand, one can find Muslims in the diaspora who struggle for secularization and declare that it is only because of secularization in the Western world that there is freedom to live as Muslims in European countries, sometimes more than in Islamic countries. According to the Islamic Council in Germany:

> Muslims should cooperate in associations, parties and parliaments. Only a secular state, never a religious-oriented kind of state (as it would be a Christian state), offers optimal conditions. Islam in "diaspora" needs the secular state, democracy and human rights as much as air for breathing.[2]

To find a common ground for discussions, we must recognize that two things are often mixed: a more material issue and a process of ideas, two streams that must be observed and evaluated separately.

1. Since the middle of the 17th century, secularization has weakened the economic position of European churches, with their property being

handed over to the state or "secularized".[3] In reality this meant expropriation. At the beginning of the 19th century, in the so-called secularization, the German Roman Catholic Church lost four archbishoprics, 18 bishoprics and about 300 abbeys and monasteries (their landed property was equal to about 70,000 sq.km.). The Protestant churches lost a third of this amount. The political power of the clergy was destroyed by this, but cultural treasures were also destroyed in the same way. Similar accounts could be cited from other European countries (for example, during the French Revolution in 1789).

Muslim writer Bassam Tibbi, who teaches in Germany, observes that this episode in European history has an impact on the Muslim world as well:

> In modern European history, the Peace of Westphalia in 1648 marked the decay of the divine order and the emergence of the modern international system of sovereign states. At its outset, this system was restricted to Europe. In the aftermath of the French Revolution national sovereignty emerged as the legitimating device of the states participating in this system. In the three hundred years following the Peace of Westphalia, Europeans imposed this system of states, each enjoying internal and external sovereignty, on the rest of the world, including the Muslim part of it. The new nation-states in the world of Islam, as much as in the other parts of the so-called Third World, are however *nominal* nation-states, because they lack the substance of a *real* nation-state.[4]

2. In addition to this "material" loss of property, the church lost its influence in the cultural and political realms. Originally religious codes of conduct lost their religious character and became "worldly", secular.[5] This led to a new understanding in politics and other areas. The social and economic process of industrialization and urbanization pushed secularization in this sense forward. The traditional unity of living and working declined and broke down. Primary social groups like family and neighbourhood, which were the points of contact for the church, lost their importance.

It is evident that this could happen only when the church was in a weak position. Thus secularization is not an invention of the church during a time of power, but a sign of defeat. Because of this, the churches long resisted the results of this process.

To understand the process of development up to this stage one must go back to the starting point. When it began in the time of Jesus' preaching and teaching, the Christian faith was not in a position of power. The Christian community regarded itself as the bearer of a message received by Jesus which it was the duty of all Christians to deliver. In this message of Jesus the kingdom of God is no political empire. It is an active but at the same time hidden reality. To explain this Jesus used the parable of the seed growing secretly:

> Jesus also said, "The Kingdom of God is as if someone would scatter seed on the ground, and would sleep and rise night and day, and the seed would sprout and grow, he does not know how. The earth produces of itself, first the stalk, then the head, then the full grain in the head. But when the grain is ripe, at once he goes in with his sickle, because the harvest has come" (Mark 4:26-29).

The kingdom of God does not mean a politico-national order of society, but something quite different, which can be brought about only by God himself. The kingdom of God is a gift of God, a total renewal of the world. Believers must act according to the rules of the kingdom of God, but they are not promised that they will get it in hand.

That there was a difference between the kingdom of God and any form of state was emphasized by Jesus, who said, "My kingdom is not from this world" (John 18:36) and "Give to the emperor things that are the emperor's and to God the things that are God's" (Mark 12:17). As an effect of this, the Christian community remained a minority, even a persecuted minority, in the state of Rome. Not until the Edict of Milan in 313 were there links between the church and the political powers. Only at the end of the 4th century did the church become the imperial church or established church. The Christian faith then became the state religion. In the course of time, the church became an organization similar to the state. Its power grew to the point that rivalry broke out between church and state. Sometimes the state ruled the church; at other times the representative of the state had to show his obedience to the power of the church, as was done in the pilgrimage to Canossa of Henry IV in 1077 (Gregory the Great). The power of the church operated not only in political affairs but in all realms of life. Scholarly work was possible only in the framework of the teaching of the church. All scientific and intellectual endeavour had to serve theology, which was the mother of all sciences.

Structures and dogmas

This background must be taken into account when discussing secularization. It must be borne in mind that the power of the medieval *Western* church was not the power of single persons, but the power of dogmas and dogmatic systems. Because of this, secularization is directed not only at hierarchical structures but also at the power of ideas based on dogmas. The insistence that dogma not interfere with science made possible new endeavours in this field.

According to Friedhelm Büttner,

> in Europe secularization is understood as an historical process which started in the age of the renaissance and in the course of which more and more fields deviated from a solely religious-based norm: separation of throne and altar, science without regard for clerical/ecclesiastical dogmas, a tendency to base almost everything in politics, science and culture on human, profane and worldly ways. For many, secularization has become a category of progress, of historically necessary development. The philosophers have reduced theology to anthropology (Feuerbach). Religion lost its character as the ultimate resort of meaning.[6]

Religion — strictly speaking, the Christian faith — was no longer the norm, but rational thinking which led to pluralistic systems.

> Perhaps this sounds a bit strange to Muslims. It may be that the real achievements of the European Enlightenment and the ensuing secularization, namely the de-secularizing of church and the de-clericalization of political powers, are irrelevant to Islam. The dualism of clerical or religious and secular realms has been characteristic of Europe, it could be said, but not of the world of Islam. An Islamic equivalent of "church" does not exist; therefore, there is nothing to be "secularized" in Islam. Muslims today perceive the threat from the West not in secularism as a contradiction to sacred or religious matters, not in science, industrialization, engineering or technology, but in un-Islamic values connected with them, that is, the pluralism and scepticism of Western society.[7]

But all these items belong together. Liberation from religious influence could not be restricted only to parts of human thinking, acting and behaving. So the values and the moral code had to be elaborated anew.

It must be emphasized that secularization affected both sides: the Western European churches lost their secular influence and power and were restricted to religious affairs in the sense of pastoral care, worship services and the like; at the same time, the state and the political powers lost their religious façade and had to act without religious sanctions. But secularization is more than a matter of relations between church and state. It is a process of detaching human codes of conduct, social order, ethical claims and cultural achievements from the religious grounds in which they originated. Secularization is the process by which all these items become purely worldly or profane matters.

The age of Enlightenment led to broad acceptance of the connection of reason and conscience, and the motto of the French revolution, "liberty, equality and fraternity", came into wide use. At the centre of the problem of secularization was freedom and its limitations.[8] Already in the early 16th century Martin Luther wrote in *Von der Freiheit eines Christenmenschen* (1520): "A Christian is at the same time a free lord over all things, subject to none, and a ministering servant of all things, subject to everyone." Although this was before secularization in the strict sense began, it is one of its roots. Luther did not agree with the church's teaching of his time. He used the freedom to interpret the Holy Scriptures in a new way. But for him freedom was limited in the Christian faith. Later, the problem became whether freedom in a secularized form preserves its religious grounds in itself or whether it loses it and even changes it to the contrary. At this time, the problem of tolerance arose.

Secularization is not atheistic, but stresses the plurality of views. Categories of secularization are rationality, critical intelligence, scientific consistency, intellectual independence. Secularization can have negative results. For example, withdrawal from religious patronage can lead to new dependencies and "faithful" affirmation of new authorities. In this way ideas which seemed to have been overcome return in a new form. Modern ideologies are in a sense religiously "charged", full of new religious moments. Christian resistance to the consequences of secularization often meant opposition to the whole concept of secularization. Later, Western churches learned to acknowledge and even appreciate the good fruits of secularization.

Christians do not have to defend or justify secularization. In the beginning there were many attacks on this idea by the churches; and in our time we see clearly the many defects and failures that surround secularization when it becomes an ideology. So the task remains to describe distinctively the aspects of secularism which we see in a positive way.

It took some time to find a positive approach to secularization. German theologian Friedrich Gogarten argued after the second world war for "secularization" as a legitimate consequence of Christian faith, paving the way for a new evaluation of humanity and the world. But even in the 1950s it was possible to write in a well-known theological dictionary: "The notion 'secularization' characterizes this process as an event which should not have occurred."

The stance of churches on religious freedom, for instance, emerged only in the middle of the 20th century. At its first assembly in 1948, the

World Council of Churches adopted a declaration on religious freedom. In the Roman Catholic Church, it was only the Second Vatican Council in 1965 which brought the important change of basically acknowledging human rights, including religious freedom. The concept of tolerance, which prevailed until then, was quite a different notion. Tolerance (instead of respect) had been practised in graduated ways and did not at all mean freedom. In the background was the concept of truth, which could not allow error or heresy.

When one begins with God as Creator of all human beings and with Jesus Christ as the mediator of salvation for all, this means a universal message for all people, giving a dignity and a vocation to every single person. In this way the Christian message of truth includes the acceptance of other persons. At the same time, it includes the claim for justice. Therefore Christians can struggle authentically for the truth only when they stand up at the same time for freedom and work for reconciliation.

In this way secularization has become a challenge for the Western churches to find a way back to their own roots. One of these basics comes from the description of Christ Jesus in the letter of Paul to the Philippians: Jesus "emptied himself, taking the form of a slave, being born in human likeness. And being found in human form, he humbled himself and became obedient to the point of death, even death on a cross" (2:7-8).

Secularization resists admiring the human being as God or as an infallible being. It recognizes the limits of human rationality and knows the insufficiency of political and social systems. With this insufficiency in mind, it searches for improvements and reforms, aims at a better, more humane and genuinely just world.

NOTES

1 Angelika Hartmann, "Der unbekannte Islam", *Zeitwende*, 1993, p.25.

2 "Islam und Grundgesetz", *Moslemische Revue*, no. 1, 1992, pp.10-15, quoting a declaration of the German branch of the Islamic World Congress, 24 September 1989.

3 Cf. Ludwig Hagemann, *Christentum: Für das Gespräch mit Muslimen*, Altenberge, CIS Verlag, 1984, p.25.

4 Bassam Tibbi, "Major Themes in the Arabic Political Literature of Islamic Revivalism, 1970-1985", *Islam and Christian/Muslim Relations*, 1992, p.188.

5 Hagemann, *op. cit.*, p.25.

6 Friedhelm Büttner, "Ist der Säkularismus eine Chance für die Christen in den Staaten und Gesellschaften des Nahen Ostens?" (unpublished manuscript).

7 Hartmann, *op. cit.*, p.25.

8 "Säkularisierung", in *Evangelisches Soziallexikon*, Stuttgart, Kreuz, 7th ed., 1980, col. 1101.

Part IV

13. Secularism and Religion

Alternative Bases for the Quest for a Genuine Pluralism

BERT F. BREINER

Alternative worldviews

It is always dangerous to make too sharp a dichotomy between secularism and religion, particularly if it results in a tendency for people of different religions to form a common alliance "over against" secularism. Religious believers need to rethink some of their basic assumptions about secularism; otherwise, a genuine dialogue between religious faith and secularism will be difficult if not impossible, hampering human cooperation in a world which manifestly needs as much of it as possible.

Yet the difference between secularism and religious faith is real and profound. There is a struggle between them in the modern world, and this cannot be ignored or easily explained away. Before examining this struggle, however, there is a vocabulary problem. I want to argue that religious faith and secularism are "alternative worldviews". The problem is that "worldview" is too static a concept. What really needs to be stressed are the dynamic implications of these alternative stances which people may assume towards the world. It is said that Archimedes, when he discovered the mathematics of the lever, exclaimed: "Give me a place to stand (*poú stō*) and I will move the earth". One could say that religion and secularism each offers an alternative *poú stō*, a base from which to seek to affect the course of history, in order to change, to move, the world.

The complex of ideas surrounding the Arabic words for religion and faith reflect the dynamic I am speaking about. The word usually translated "religion" (*Dīn*) covers a semantic range which includes religion, judgment and conduct. These apparently diverse meanings actually reflect a particular understanding of the true significance of religion in human life. "Religion" implies not just a set of beliefs, but a *way of behaving* in the world; and this in turn reflects the values upon which people make the decisions, the *judgments*, of everyday life. Of course, religion rests ultimately on faith (*Imān*), faith that the values and understanding upon which a religious system is based are ultimately trustworthy and true. The root of *Imān* implies "security, firmness" and ultimately refers to a deep conviction that a particular system of values or worldview is worth staking your life on. Faith is the conviction that we have a secure basis for facing the large and the small, the ordinary and the extraordinary choices and decisions we are called upon to make.

The English word "religion", on the other hand, has a very different etymology, which is also revealing. It derives ultimately from the Latin *re-ligare* meaning "to bind back" or "to bind together again". These two possible meanings of the original Latin word reflect important dimensions of religious faith. Religious faith binds us back to the ultimate origin and goal of all life, to the source of all meaning. It holds together all the disparate and often seemingly contradictory realities and experiences of life in a coherent whole. Unfortunately, the etymology of the word is not as transparent to speakers of English as the etymology of *Dīn* and *Imān* are to speakers of Arabic. I would, therefore, like to borrow a word from the New Testament which bespeaks this fundamental understanding of religion. Today's English Version translates Colossians 1:17 as follows: "Christ existed before all things, and in union with him all things have their proper place." The same thought is expressed again in Ephesians 1:10. Paul uses a Greek word to describe this reality which may be translated "sums up" or "recapitulates". This is an important function of religious faith. It "recapitulates" reality in the system of faith and practice which is present to the believer as a firm basis for living.

Of course, this is equally true of secularism. It too rests on a system of values which is believed to be an appropriate basis for decision and action in everyday life. There is equally an element of faith in the adequacy of the understanding of the world thus presented. Like religious faith, secularism attempts to recapitulate all the dimensions of human life and so to sum them up into a meaningful system of belief and action. And just as there are many religions in the world, so too there are many alternative "secularisms", with different norms and values and different philosophical constructs to match. Where then are we to look for the difference between secularism and religious faith?

The essential difference between secularism and religious faith, I would argue, is that secularism believes that the world in which we live may be understood entirely in its own terms. There is no need to refer to any other point of reference in order to understand its meaning and its value. From it we can understand our own purpose and function within it and derive the values which will enable us to fulfil our proper role in the universe. Religious faith, on the other hand, insists that the true meaning and value of life in this world, indeed of the universe as a whole, can be discerned only by reference to some reality which is transcendent to the whole of the universe. It is this element of transcendence which unites all forms of religious faith, theistic and non-theistic, in distinction from the secularist worldview.

Religion (in all its variety) and secularism (in all its variety) are then two alternative ways of recapitulating the meaning and value of all things within a coherent system of beliefs, values and practices. They are two radically different recapitulations of reality, for they differ on the very point of reference necessary to bring order to the seeming chaos of human experience and the natural world. For secularism the universe in which we live provides its own ultimate source of reference. It is intelligible and manageable *on its own terms*. For religious faith, life in this universe is ultimately intelligible and so needs to be managed in reference to a reality which is *transcendent to it*.

This difference between secularism and religion is one of the most important aspects of the quest for a genuine form of pluralism in contemporary societies throughout the world — the struggle of nations and peoples everywhere successfully to bring together, recapitulate, all the dimensions, differences and commonalities of human experience into a harmonious relationship with their own diversity and with the even greater diversity of the natural world which is the necessary matrix of all human life as we know it.

In the final analysis, the struggle between religious and secular recapitulations of reality may be reduced to a fundamental disagreement over the ultimate point of reference for human values and for the appropriate criteria for human action. Does this ultimate point of reference lie within or beyond the universe in which we live? The current debate among physicists about the Third Law of Thermodynamics (the Law of Entropy) is illustrative. According to this law, the natural inclination of the natural order is to proceed in the direction of chaos and dissolution. For order and cohesion to exist there must be a source of energy which comes from outside the system. In the case of life on earth, this source of energy is the sun, which is turned into energy basically through the action of green plants, hence the traditional importance of fossil fuels. Of course, the power of the sun may be harnessed in a variety of other ways such as windmills and solar energy batteries. Today nuclear fission and fusion provide alternative sources of energy. But traditionally the Law of Entropy stated clearly that the natural state of the universe was towards its own destruction in eventual chaos.

The current debate over the validity of the Law of Entropy has led many modern physicists to develop a number of metaphysical theories about the nature and origin of the universe. This return of metaphysics to the very pinnacle of contemporary science is in itself an important and interesting development, but the basic question for the modern world is the essence of this debate: are the natural order and the place of humanity within it intelligible without reference to a transcendent reality? In many ways, the "soft" sciences like sociology and economics have not caught up with the changing scientific concerns of the "hard" sciences. They are not yet seriously considering whether or not their disciplines need to be grounded in a transcendent reality beyond the human experience and the world in which it exists.

The religious recapitulation of reality suddenly finds itself more in line with contemporary hard science than do the many social sciences, which have long claimed to share a common worldview with the classical empiricism of the "scientific worldview". Religious faith speaks to the same metaphysical concerns that physicists are increasingly addressing in the modern world. This raises some interesting questions about the future of the human quest for an adequate understanding of life in the world and so of life in society.

Interconnectedness and individualism

We are becoming increasingly aware that humanity is facing a crisis. There is the natural crisis of the increasing pollution of the world in which we live, of the dangers which attend our mastery of the atom and of the other secrets of nature, of the fragility of the natural world of which we are a part. There is also growing awareness of a human crisis. Its nature is perhaps not new: history is full of suffering, wars, hunger and inequality, and there is nothing new about human selfishness and greed. One might argue that the scale of it is more dramatic today than at other times in history, but I do not think that that is the source of the modern malaise.

Increasingly, humanity is becoming aware of the interconnectedness of reality, of "ecology", of the natural interconnectedness of all life-forms on the planet, of the interdependence which binds all human societies together in ever tighter relationships. We can no longer solve our problems without reference to others. North and South are no longer separable spheres of human life and experience. The result of all of this is, I believe, to call into question the adequacy of the individualism which has so long dominated the Western understanding of the human condition.

Western secularism is bound up with an individualistic understanding of the human person. This does not mean that it is unaware of the social dimension of human life. Secular humanists have taught us recently to be concerned about economic injustice on a global scale and have pointed to the relationship between economic policies in the comparatively affluent North and poverty in the more or less dependent South. Nevertheless, the fundamental category of Western humanism remains the individual. Its concept of human rights is clearly based on the idea of the individual. The legal fiction of a corporation as a "person" or "individual" before the law reflects the fundamental categories of Western thought. Even Western concepts of socialism are ultimately couched in terms of the individual: "the greatest good for the greatest number". The ultimate reference of social value is found in the number of individuals who benefit from the structures and programmes of society as a whole.

It is not surprising, therefore, that Western secularism has found it difficult to deal with the reality of communalism in different parts of the world. In the former Yugoslavia, in Sudan, in the Indian sub-continent, communalism is challenging the very basis on which the Western concept of democracy rests: the primacy of the individual in the life of society. Western law rarely recognizes the rights or obligations of communities of persons except, as we have noted, under the legal fiction of a treating of the corporation as an individual under the law. Nor is it only in Asia, Africa and Eastern Europe that one must look for the problems which attend the individualism of Western secularism. The inability of modern secular societies to deal with communal identity is inherent in the many forms of discrimination which the law must seek to address. Racism, sexism, discrimination on the basis of language, culture or religion present serious problems throughout the Western world.

It has been argued that religion cannot serve as the basis for a modern society. A common argument is that history proves that religions tend naturally towards intolerance. In fact, there were periods in history when religious states provided levels of tolerance and an integration of different religious communities which equal or surpass the accomplishments of modern secular society. Modern secular society has not proved able to eliminate the myriad forms of discrimination which we read about in the papers and which we know from our own experience.

There is, I believe, no longer a high level of confidence in the ability of the Western secular worldview to bring justice to masses of men and women in the world today. It seems unable to cope with the reality of communal identity. Communal identity does not, on the other hand, look like it is on the verge of disappearing. Even in Western Europe it never died. Danish, Dutch, German, Friesian, Walloon, Vlaams, Basque, Catalan, Welsh, Scottish, Irish — these identities did not die within the modern nation-state and they certainly do not look like they are about to in the near future. When we move outside Western Europe the list seems endless — Serb, Croat, Moldavian, Kurd, Panjabi, Tutsi, Hutu, Tibetan...

The need for integration

The problem facing the modern world is primarily how to integrate many different value systems, social systems and communal identities into one society — to recapitulate a large variety of recapitulations. I would argue that the religious worldview is, potentially, in a better position to do so than is the secularist worldview. I believe this is true for three reasons: (1) the fact that the religious recapitulation is not self-contained but by definition has a transcendent reference; (2) the fact that religion has been forced to confront its own weakness in the light of the humanist critique of religious faith over the last few centuries; (3) the experience of the world's religions in what is often called "spiritual formation". Of course, these three resources do not guarantee that the religious worldview will provide an integrative role for society, only that religion in the contemporary world is *potentially* able to do so because of the resources that it has available to it.

It may seem ironic that the transcendent reference of the religious recapitulation should be the first resource listed for religious faith to use in developing a pluralistic worldview. After all, this transcendent reference (God, in the theistic religions) has often been identified as a source of religious intolerance. Nor is this difficult to understand. Since this absolute reference is transcendent to the whole of the created order, it is ultimately self-verifying and cannot easily be challenged by any lesser considerations.

But religious experience shows that this is not necessarily the case. An acute awareness of the transcendent reference of religious faith may also lead to a realization that even revealed religion does not exhaust the reality of that transcendence. This has given rise to the "negative theology" found in aspects of Jewish, Christian and Muslim thought and the "*neti, neti*" ("Not that! Not that!") of the Eastern traditions. Although most positively and consistently developed in the mystical traditions of the world's religions, this "negative theology" of transcendence is available to the tradition as whole. Understood in this light, the transcendent reference of religious faith could as readily become a basis for tolerance as intolerance. This contrasts sharply with the secularist worldview. The secularist conviction that the world is intelligible on its own terms leads to the conclusion that, given a sufficient knowledge of the world, one could potentially find and state the truth absolutely in human language. The religious believer should be protected from this form of hubris because he or she knows that God is always "greater" than anything that can be known or stated by the human mind.

Second, the humanist critique of religious faith over the last few centuries has obliged religion to confront both its fundamental assumptions about the authority of the transcendent and its facile attempts to convert this into a this-worldly absolutism. The absolutism into which contemporary religious movements fall is, I believe, different from the absolutism of religious faith in previous periods of history. Today religious absolutism ("fundamentalism") is often found among those who have had a secular education and have not been trained in the traditional religious sciences: engineers, chemists, sociologists. They tend to accept the basically secular premise that human experience and reason provide a sufficient resource for understanding the meaning of the human condition. They differ from traditional secularism only in accepting the data of revealed religion as a meaningful part of the knowledge data base of human experience.

Traditionally, it was the ultimately transcendent nature of the focus of religious belief that gave it its "other-worldly" character. Although usually a pejorative description of traditional religious belief, "other-worldliness" was an important element in providing a potentially liberating and open view of systems of faith and belief in this world. History tells us that religion did often develop a high level of tolerance in different times and places. When it did not, it may be because the relative hegemony of one particular system of belief in a given time and place made it easy to obscure the transcendent reference of faith. It seemed so completely the common property of men and women in a given society that its reference beyond the immediate life of the community of faith was often obscured.

In any case, traditional religious faith has had to look at itself in the light of modern secularism. It is helpful for anyone's self-understanding to see oneself through another's eyes. Secularism, until very recently anyway, has not been forced to see itself through any eyes other than its own.

In the final analysis, we are not speaking about systems of values or disembodied beliefs with a life of their own, nor even about God, for God in the glorious transcendence and self-sufficient reality of the divine transcendence is not the object of religious knowledge. True, the divine self may be the ultimate object of religious faith and the source of all religious knowledge, but religion is what binds all of us and all of creation both "together again" and "back" to God. In the end, both secularist and religious believer are talking about men and women, people, human beings and their life in the world.

For the modern secularist, education is central. People need to be educated in order to understand the world, human society and their place within it. If there was ever a truly gnostic religion, it is this deep, almost unquestioning belief of modern secularism in knowledge as the key to a better world and to a better life. And yet when one looks at the curriculum of modern secularism, where is a person to be formed in terms of values and personal commitment to the higher ideals and aspirations of society? Chemistry and physics, literature and mathematics, sociology and history — all have a place in the curriculum. What is lacking in the curriculum in most systems are courses in ethics and philosophy.

Religious formation, on the other hand, deals with questions of ethics and moral philosophy. If religion in the world today could develop its ability not to absolutize any earthly system (including religion), then a firm spiritual formation could provide the world with what it needs the most: men and women who are secure in their identity, bound firmly back (*religio*) to the ultimate reference and goal of human life and yet prevented from a too facile absolutism by the transcendent reference of the ultimate reality for which they long and in obedience to which they live.

Part IV

14. State, Religion and Laïcité: The Western European Experience

JØRGEN S. NIELSEN

We in Western Europe tend to have a sadly short historical perspective. This is one reason why the English find it so difficult to deal with the Irish question and why the Western European understanding of what is going on in the former Yugoslavia is so much shallower than that, for example, of many Turks. But if we are to learn to deal with the challenges presented to our accustomed way of doing things in public, social and cultural life by the Muslim communities now settled among us (communities that are here because we needed them at a certain time for short-term economic considerations), we must review our own history. In so doing we shall discover that there is nothing absolutely right about how we organize ourselves. Through this discovery there is hope that we may be able to struggle into a future which also allows Muslim communities room to discover where they fit in as partners in a common plural society and enables us, the "old communities", to see not a threat but an opportunity.

One area in which the presence of Muslim communities over the last few decades has put pressure on our accustomed traditions has been in the relationship between religion and state. For several centuries this was the arena in which many European wars were fought, but most of us had probably concluded that this question was now confined to the history books. The challenge has been reinforced in the last few years by the collapse of the accustomed order in Eastern Europe, where it has turned out that the old European tensions of nation, religion and state have not in fact been solved but only suppressed. The presence of a new generation of Muslims in Western Europe ensures that the question has been retrieved from the history books and reinserted into public debate.

It is therefore quite appropriate to review where we have come from. This will involve a survey of the historical unfolding of church-state relations and then a more detailed consideration of where we arrived as a result. Finally, we shall look at where Muslims fit into this situation in terms of the conceptions they bring with them, the adaptations which have already taken place and the further adaptations which need to be considered.

The European heritage

The Christianization of Europe was a slow and often painful process. Only in the 11th and 12th centuries was the process anywhere near completion in the West, and that was achieved in part by the suppression of the traditions of Celtic Christianity, which had played an important role in the early Christianization of Northern Europe, as far inland as Aachen (Aix-la-Chapelle). A central element of the political structure of Western Europe, which arose in this period, was the unity of sovereign and subjects in one church. Treason and heresy were two sides of the same coin; blasphemy was a threat to the secular order as much as it was to the divine order. The sovereign ruled *Dei gratia* — or, as later absolutist theory put it, by divine right.

Although this unity was only seldom challenged internally, it was not without its tensions in the wider world. For this was also the period when the papacy was asserting the supremacy of the Bishop of Rome over mere earthly monarchs. Tension between the kings' ambitions and those of the church was constant. In its purest form high feudal theory saw the pope as the supreme earthly lord to whom kings paid homage. Only on the basis of this homage could the kings legitimately in turn be paid homage by their fief holders, and so on down a strict hierarchy. The balance between the two sides was never stable. Occasionally, quite powerful kings had to succumb to papal authority, while at other times Rome grudgingly accepted what amounted to the autonomy of the king and the church in a given region.

While it introduced new theological concepts into this field, the Reformation did not of itself cause a major change — certainly not immediately. In those states which adopted the Reformation the old tensions between royal authority and the papal claim to supreme authority disappeared, which was one reason many monarchs welcomed the Reformation. Otherwise, the model remained the unity of sovereign and subjects in the one religion organized through the one church. The sovereign was granted religious legitimacy by the church in exchange for guaranteeing its hierarchy and its legal and material interests — although this was obviously not always the main theological explanation favoured.

This was affirmed in the 1648 Treaty of Westphalia, ending the Thirty Years War, in the principle of *cuius regio eius religio*: to each state its religion.

But by this time, however, the seeds were already being planted for the breaching of the tradition. Within a year of Westphalia, the English civil war ended with the execution of a monarch who had tried to hold together the state by a religion which large sections of the population disliked. The Restoration of the monarchy in 1660 came about only on the basis of an agreement to tolerate a certain degree of religious plurality — in the form of Protestant dissent, though not yet reconstituted Roman Catholicism. Likewise, in the Low Countries a new tradition of religious pluralism was becoming established. Transported across the Atlantic this tradition of dissent laid the foundations for what became a century later the United States of America. But there, too, episodes of repression of religious minorities occurred, even after the adoption of the constitution.

More profound changes were also rooted in the generations immediately following Westphalia. By the end of the 17th century we discern the first signs of what historians have called the period of enlightened despotism. Both parts of the term — "enlightened" and "despotism" — are significant. The movement of the Enlightenment and the *philosophes* gradually extended the intellectual space within which it was possible to move without authorization from the church. French writers and thinkers played a prominent role in this trend, but it was not confined to Catholic countries, as is attested by the work of experimental scientists in various parts of the continent and the spread of bourgeois themes in the arts. The struggle was tense and the balance between the church and the secular shifted regularly. The church and its defenders were reluctant to surrender the field of empirical and experimental science, as was evidenced over the years from Galileo to Darwin.

The key issue was not primarily one of religious belief, but of ecclesiastical authority. For the church the danger lay not in the astronomical question of the centre of the universe or the debate about evolution. At the core was the question of authority. And as the church lost its authority, the state had to find alternative pillars on which to rest its own authority.

In many states, this was welcomed, at least in the short term, by the sovereigns, who had regularly shown impatience at how the church restrained and limited their freedom of movement. Again there was little difference here between Protestant and Catholic Europe, except in the particular institutional and political processes and the language in which the relationship might be expressed. The attraction of the despotism of the monarchy to the 18th-century kings was not purely self-aggrandizement and enrichment. It was seen as a tool for eliminating old-fashioned "power centres" — guilds, nobility, feudal lords, corporations and above all the church — in order to increase the wealth of the nation (a word which became popular at this time) to the benefit of all the subjects, each according to his station, of course, but still to the benefit of all.

Certainly some sovereigns exploited this theory cynically, but many appear to have had sincere convictions about their policies. The trouble with this combination of enlightenment and despotism was that while the former encouraged people to think for themselves, the latter gave them the material incentive to do so, and in the process to abolish these traditional institutions which stood in the way of autonomous thought and material incentive.

The extreme synthesis of these elements was the chain of events leading to the French Revolution and laying the foundations for models to be developed through the 19th and into the 20th century. Of general relevance across Europe was the principle of the revolution that sovereignty lay with the people, the *demos* of the ancient Greeks, although more broadly defined than they had envisaged. Of direct relevance to Catholic states was the deeply emotional and sometimes violent anti-clericalism, which has continued to haunt nation-state ideologies in countries of Catholic tradition, even though it was very soon tempered by the concordat model negotiated by Napoleon — the magnanimous, though still self-interested, victory of the sovereign over the papacy.

Although the most prominent clashes during this period were in Catholic countries, Protestant states were not immune to the tensions building up between the new ideas of the Enlightenment and institutions of learning and the church, but they did not generally lead to major public clashes. The churches in Protestant states tended to be subservient to and dependent on the state, and any ideas of an alternative scenario were decisively undermined by the experience of Napoleonic occupation or protectorate. The roots of national independence, as the 19th century progressed in the regions affected by French expansion, lay in asserting a distinction from the populism and anti-clericalism of the revolutionary models imposed by Napoleonic imperialism. So we see in the middle of the century the romantic-national movements of central Europe and Scandinavia, which re-created and mythologized pre-Christian tribal-national roots of nationhood which were not necessarily democratic.

As the authority of the church weakened and the state began to find alternative sources of legitimacy, wider and wider sectors of society and culture developed their own foundations of legitimacy. The natural sciences and the new and growing social sciences developed their own self-confirming rationales of "objective" scientific methods based on observation, experimentation and categorization. This did not necessarily make scientists atheists; many clearly remained committed believers. But they no longer needed the church or its theology to provide the intellectual authorization for what they were doing. Belief was increasingly seen as little more than a matter of personal commitment. The church continued to be one of the main factors holding society together, but the geographical and social mobility brought about by industrialization and urbanization was also weakening the church in that function.

In response new religious movements arose to fill the gaps. In Britain they tended to take the form of new non-conformist churches, the best example being the Methodist Church. Elsewhere movements appeared on the fringes of the church — such as pietist and evangelical movements — and then infiltrated into the mainstream. Some of these had a strong authoritarian streak in their organization, but they held in common a growing emphasis on the place of individual commitment, even conversion.

There was no longer any consensus on the relationship between belief, institutional church and Christianity in the social and political life of the nation. On the one hand were strongly secularist and laicist trends in the intellectual world and politics, often associated with anti-clericalism. Not only was religion seen as a matter of personal belief, but its institutional expression was to be confined to the private domain by a complete disengagement of church or religion and state. This found its most formal expression in France in 1905. On the other hand, especially in Protestant Europe, an important sector of society saw a need to retain some form of tie between the nation and its Christian heritage, expressed in some form of continuing relationship between religion and state. It is perhaps not coincidental that it is in the Catholic countries, where anticlericalism and laicism tended to be strongest, that the reaction of the church and its adherents tended to find expression in the form of Christian political parties.

At various times these developments gave rise to major political or cultural crises, such as the *Kulturkampf* in Bismarck's imperial Germany, but generally most of Western Europe had reached a reasonably comfortable *modus vivendi* by the early part of the 20th century. This comfortable feeling was temporarily shattered by the experience of fascist supremacy during the 1930s and 1940s. The often too-cosy relationship between established churches and fascist or Nazi dictatorships in Italy, Spain and Germany provoked the formation of politically dissident church movements in those countries, as well as in the countries which came under German occupation. Cleaning up the mess after 1945 was often painful. But in a sense the whole episode came to be regarded as an aberration; and post-war settlements were designed to confirm and reinforce the earlier arrangements, but amended in ways to prevent such an aberration occurring again.

There was little serious questioning of the main features of the constitutional ordering of church-state relations which had been achieved by the early part of the present century. Such questioning arose only much later as new religious minorities entered the scene. But before considering this development and its consequences, it might be useful to take stock of the situation as we have inherited it today.

The current situation

The system of church-state relations in Western Europe today has remained remarkably unchanged over the last century and retains surprisingly large elements from the historical background sketched above:

1. The continuing process of alienation of people from the church is clearly not a new phenomenon. Linked to it is a new phase of fringe Christian movements, which is leading in some countries to the establishment of new churches, while in other countries the existing churches are being infiltrated, for example, by charismatics, house churches, "New Age" ideas and the like.

2. Much of the outward expression of church-state relations, especially in the monarchies, is strongly infused with elements from the time of princes.

3. Perhaps most remarkably, *cuius regio eius religio* still seems to prevail, even if not *de jure*. To all intents and purposes, only the United Kingdom and the Netherlands are truly multi-denominational countries. Germany is multi-denominational only because the separate states of the 1648 Westphalia settlement have since come together, but each of the territories of the states of 1648 is today still essentially characterized by the particular denomination which prevailed then. The same can be said of the cantons of Switzerland.

However, each state has developed different traditions, so that the particular situation in each country differs in one or another important aspect. Nevertheless, one can identify enough common traits to suggest three main types.

The first is a *laicist* type, with separation between church or religion and state. Total separation does not exist in practice, even where it may exist in law. France is the main example of this type, but public funding for church schools — and for the Paris mosque since the 1920s — as well as the system of chaplains in the army and the prisons detracts from the purity of the separation. Separation of church and state has not necessarily arisen out of an anti-clerical tradition such as that of France. The Netherlands has been moving quite deliberately in this direction over the last decades, and a few Swiss cantons could also be cited. The Republic of Ireland also has a constitutional separation of church and state.

A second model, the Napoleonic precedent of a *concordat* with the church, prevails in a few countries, such as Italy, Spain and Portugal. Like the laicist states, such countries have traditionally been Roman Catholic. But this model seems to have become increasingly dysfunctional. Spain has been moving away from it since the re-establishment of the constitutional monarchy; and the discrediting of the old political parties in Italy, especially the Christian Democrats, may very well lead that country away from the concordat tradition as well.

The third and most widespread pattern remains some form of domestically arranged *establishment*. This appears in two forms: *recognition* by the state of a special status for certain churches or religious communities and *incorporation* of a church into the constitutional structure of the state in some form. Recognition does not always mean the same thing. Many Swiss cantons operate with a form of recognition, as do Germany, Austria, Belgium and the three Alsace-Mosel departments ceded to France by Germany after the 1914-18 war. In Germany the main effect is that the state collects a church tax on behalf of the churches; in Belgium and Alsace-Mosel recognition means state funding of clergy and religious education; in Austria access to the public broadcast media also goes with recognition.

The incorporation form of establishment has traditionally existed in its most pure form in Scandinavia, especially in Denmark where the Lutheran state church is a government ministry without even any form of synod to give it an element of institutional existence distinguishable from the state. But other varieties abound. In Britain there is separation of church and state in Wales and Northern Ireland, although very close cooperation in education through church schools; while in England the Anglican church is "established", with particular privileges, and other churches have different statuses; and in Scotland the relationship between the Presbyterian church and the state is again different (although in both England and Scotland the monarch is formally the head of the church).

In some countries establishment takes place under a general legal category, to which particular denominations can be added. Thus in Germany, the various churches recognized in a *Land* are all subject to the same general legislation, as is the case also in Belgium. In England, on the other hand, each of the major denominations has its own specific legislation and unique position. Thus when the English Congregationalists, Presbyterians and Church of Christ wished to come together in the United Reformed Church in 1972, a special act of parliament was required.

Some countries straddle types and can move from one to another. Spain seems to be moving from concordat to establishment by recognition. Norway, Sweden and Denmark, all with incorporated state churches, also extend one or another form of recognition to religious denominations other than the state church.

A place for Muslims?

The current situation in Western Europe is both complicated and deeply rooted in political and constitutional structures and national cultures. It has grown out of a particular history whose results often represent a compromise between rival forces. But the parties to the compromise were all actors in the history, and even though one or another may not be too pleased with the outcome, they understand it and know how to live with it, even manipulate it to their own advantage.

The same cannot be said for newcomers into the system. They must first unlearn their own expectations and then learn to operate in a system which is not only alien but also often against them. This is clearly the case with Muslims. In Western Europe, they have come from a variety of different histories of their own. On the face of it, their states of origin have moved in directions not dissimilar to those of Europe. This is particularly true of Turkey, with its adaptation of Western laicist models in the Kemalist system established during the 1920s. But the impact of this Westernization of institutions and constitutional arrangements was mainly in the big cities, and even so only in certain sectors of urban society. In more traditional sectors, particularly the countryside, from which most Muslim immigrants have come to Western Europe, its effects have been minimal. Religious institutions and state institutions in the Islamic world remained closely intertwined into this century.

Although the current Islamist emphasis on the congruence of religion and politics does not on the whole reflect historical reality, it does represent an important expression of traditional religious expectations and ideals.

In the countries of origin, religious institutions tended to be there because they had always been there — certainly in the countryside. The local congregation did not usually have to make a special effort to ensure the provision of basic minimum religious necessities. Only if they wanted special provision did they have to organize, as did Sufi orders and, in modern times, revival movements, to achieve goals beyond those already satisfied minimally. Muslims coming to Western European cities found no such provisions. They had to learn that even the minimum requirements needed mobilization of effort and resources, and thus organization. But the European context in which they had to achieve this presumed that other religious denominations would seek to fit in as church-like organizations. Over their long period of participation in European history Jewish communities had in fact adopted such a response. Their rabbis moved from being teachers, scholars and jurisconsults to being pastors and clergy, their synagogues became like churches and their chief rabbis like archbishops. The pressure was on for Muslims to move in the same direction.

It is noteworthy that some Muslim groups coming out of a Sufi tradition, with its often wary attitude to the political power (especially in the last couple of centuries under Western imperial power), have formally instituted themselves. In this way they were able to become visible to the agencies of the European milieu, with the purpose of mobilizing public funding in their direction. This has been the case with some success in certain British cities. Similarly, the attempts in most countries to establish some form of common Muslim front or umbrella organization is evidence of an adaptation of structures in a pseudo-ecclesiastical direction.

But ongoing links with the Muslim world have generally tended to confuse the picture both for Muslims and for European observers. These continuing connections take two forms. One, primarily associated with the early phases of migration and the first generation of migrants, refers back to the society of origin. The other, associated with the European generations, refers increasingly to the wider Islamic world, the *Ummah*. These two are not solely chronological, and one should not expect that the former phase will gradually be superseded by the second. It is more likely that they will continue to exist in some modified form parallel to and overlapping each other.

The European temptation is to demand that Muslims abandon the former and to raise question marks against the latter in terms of political implications: loyalty towards something beyond the nation or constitution, irredentism, even fifth column — at least when we are faced with military-political crises such as that of the Gulf War.

Such theoretical considerations tend to overshadow questions of what has been achieved in practice in the integration of Islam into the institutional structures of European countries. In one sense, countries with some form of establishment have had the greatest problems, mainly because they tend to have a framework of legal codes into which all newcomers must fit. When Belgium added Islam to its short list of recognized religious communities, it immediately had to adapt the administrative structure so that it was centred on the provinces rather than the smaller districts applied to the Catholic and Protestant churches, as well as to recognize the Islamic Cultural Centre in Brussels as a kind of "cathedral". Now, almost twenty years later, the consequences of recognition have been virtually nil, and much ill feeling and mistrust have been created across a spectrum of participants because of misunderstandings regarding intentions. In Germany, recognition has also been misunderstood on the Muslim side, while the official side could be accused of manipulating the system to keep the Muslims out.

Part of the problem is that participation in a highly structured system which has been developed over centuries tends to be difficult for those who come in late with a different experience. The threshold of entry required by the host institutions is thus much higher than the newcomers can reasonably be expected to manage, even when their expectations are being prematurely built up.

Here, it seems to me, the less centrally institutionalized countries have certain advantages. Above all, the threshold for entry into the system is significantly lower, and there is a more explicitly graduated route of entry. Sweden allows local voting rights to foreigners. Through its Free Church Funding Council, state funds are allocated to religious communities outside the state church, including Muslims. The Netherlands and Denmark incorporate Muslim groups also into their "free school" funding tradition. The Republic of Ireland has a Muslim member of parliament. British local governments increasingly are in partnership with local Muslim groups in a variety of practical, social programmes, and recently the Archbishop of York suggested that the next monarch should have a multifaith coronation.

Of course there are variations and exceptions within each country. Some German states, such as Berlin and Hamburg, have been in the forefront of trying to expand the limits of the possible. Equally, it has hitherto been very difficult to see a way to get a Muslim member of parliament, in contrast to the way in which Muslims have moved into local government.

With all such provisos and complications, however, one must conclude that, whatever the particular local and national situations, space is being made, sometimes reluctantly, for the Muslim presence. But this also means that as European nations begin to adapt — as they are clearly doing already — to the developing multicultural and multireligious circumstances, the new minority religions, especially Islam, will begin to influence the continuing constitutional developments as participants rather than observers or outsiders.

15. The Role of Religious Institutions and *'ulamā'* in a Contemporary Muslim Society

TAYYIB Z. AL-ABDIN

Muslims profess the comprehensive nature of Islam, which encompasses all aspects of life. Therefore, the injunctions of Islam must be the supreme criteria of human activities. However, this does not mean that religious scholars or religious institutions should run all the affairs of society. This is the logical outcome of the accepted principle that there is no formal class of clergy in Islam and that no one has the monopoly of religious interpretation or *ijtihād*.

What has supremacy are the teachings of Islam as revealed by God and expounded by the Prophet Muḥammad (PBUH), not any one institution or individual. Rulers and judges are given, within their jurisdictions, the right to choose from among multiple opinions or rulings the one which is to be binding on the citizens. Apart from these cases, the only weight a religious opinion carries is the wide acceptance it enjoys in society.

However, certain functions in modern societies are appropriately carried out by religious institutions and *'ulamā'*. We shall explain below what these functions are, what they signify and which bodies may conduct them. Examples from various Muslim countries will illustrate how these functions have actually been carried out in contemporary societies.

Prayer and rites

This function comprises congregational prayer in mosques, pilgrimage to Makkah, religious occasions such as *Mawlid al Nabī, Al Isrā' wa al Mi'rāj, 'Ashūrā', 'Īd* prayer and the like. Leading congregational prayer, especially Friday prayer, is the most important of these duties. Although any Muslim may lead the prayer, it is the common practice all over the Muslim world to assign a regular imām for each mosque.

In most Muslim countries there is a department or a ministry of religious affairs to look after the government mosques, appoint and train imāms and administer the procedure for pilgrimage. There is nothing wrong with this arrangement so long as the imām is free to give the Friday *khutbah* or *ḥalaqah* lessons according to his convictions, without interference from the government. In practice governments do intervene to avoid political criticism from the *minbar* of the mosque, which has increased in recent years as Muslim activists have started to embarrass governments on sensitive issues like the implementation of *Sharī'ah*. In countries like Egypt, Morocco, Tunisia, Iraq, Algeria and Syria, where Islamic resurgence is growing, all mosques, including private ones, have been put under strict government control. This violates the Islamic principle that an imām should not be imposed on a congregation. As a matter of fact, government imāms do not avoid politics, but speak in favour of their patron regimes.

Education

One of the earliest functions conducted by *'ulamā'* was religious education in mosques or *madrasah*. For many centuries religious education was the only education available in most Muslim countries. Secular education was established only with the advent of European colonialism. Though resisted at first, it was later accepted and adopted by Muslim governments as the major type of formal education. Religious education continued for children of 6 to 15, but attracted pupils only from poor families and rural areas.

Religious education may be entrusted to a department in the ministry of religious affairs, as in Sudan, or be under the supervision of a senior Islamic university, as in Egypt and Saudi Arabia, or be left to voluntary *'ulamā'* organizations, as in Pakistan. The best is that supervised by Islamic universities.

However, in all cases religious education is felt to be deficient in providing basic general knowledge, in qualifying the student to join the various faculties in higher education or in training him for practical life at large; and some countries are reconsidering the usefulness of a purely religious education at the primary level. In Egypt, Al Azhar, which is responsible for all religious education, has broadened the scope of its primary and secondary schools to qualify students for all types of higher education. Since 1965 Al Azhar itself has become a university of diverse specializations. Sudan went a step further by deciding in 1990 to phase out specialized religious schools and instead to increase religious instruction in common schools. The government opted for a comprehensive type of school which combines technical, religious and academic education. The student chooses one of the three specializations in the last year of the higher secondary school.

The trend is to entrust general education, including religious instruction, to persons who have been trained in faculties of education rather than to *'ulamā'* specialized in religious subjects. A similar development is taking place in higher education. The concept of an Islamic university specializing only in religious disciplines is giving way to a wider scope of branches of knowledge. The argument behind the change is that the needs of the day call for not only religious instruction but knowledgeable Muslims in all spheres of life. Some committed scholars go further, arguing that Muslims should attempt to Islamize the branches of science which they have borrowed from Western civilization. The International Institute of Islamic Thought in Washington and the Institute of Islamization of Knowledge in Sudan have been established for this purpose.

Certain conservative *'ulamā'* argue that opening an Islamic university to secular disciplines dilutes its religious character. Asked about the need to give religious orientation to trainees in other professions, they would contend that this may be pursued in secular universities if governments are serious about it. However, the self-interest of *'ulamā'* in holding senior posts in Islamic universities may be a factor behind this attitude.

Nevertheless, the religious faculties of *Sharī'ah* and *uṣūl al-dīn* (Islamic studies) remain the major units in Islamic universities catering for the training of *qāḍis*, imāms, *da'īs* (missionaries) and teachers of religious instruction. In mosques there is a role for religious instruction of adults in *ḥalaqah* lessons and of children, especially in Muslim minority communities.

Da'wah work

Da'wah work to make Muslims aware of their religious duties or to call non-Muslims to Islam was closely associated with *'ulamā'* in the past. Historically, however, many traders and soldiers played a significant role in the spread of Islam. Enjoining the good and preventing evil is a religious duty for every Muslim; and Muslims in general have a high sense of missionary work. Most ministries for religious affairs have special departments for *da'wah* work. The *'ulamā'* in these departments usually practise preaching in mosques, especially during the month of Ramaḍān.

Some organizations of an international character like Al Azhar (Egypt), the World Muslim League (Saudi Arabia) and the *Da'wah* Organization of Libya send religious instructors to Muslim minority countries during Ramaḍān. These instructors are usually graduates of departments of *da'wah* in Islamic universities. Apart from their knowledge of the Qur'ān and Sunnah, they are trained basically to deliver effective sermons in Arabic. Given their limited training and the bureaucratic manner in which they often behave, their effectiveness is limited. More serious is their close association with governments that people view as secular and unjust.

For a Muslim the religiousness of a person is judged not by his knowledge but by his piety and sincerity. Official *'ulamā'* may be respected but hardly trusted. Consequently, voluntary organizations to carry out *da'wah* work have been established in many Muslim societies. A traditional group which is quite active in this area is Jamā'at al-Tabliqh, established in India in the 1940s and specialized in spreading the elementary teachings of Islam all over the world. Initiates are asked to participate in *da'wah* for short periods (up to a year) and to avoid involvement in political matters. Although the society has hardly any *'ulamā'* at its top leadership, it is one of the most successful organizations in attracting non-practising Muslims to the fold of Islam.

Since the 1980s new types of *da'wah* organizations have emerged in Sudan, Kuwait and Saudi Arabia, which engage themselves in activities such as relief work, clinics, orphanages, schools, youth centres, adult education and even development projects. These organizations were started by Muslims educated in "non-religious" institutions, who were influenced by the effective methods used by Christian mission in Africa. Now, they are spreading elsewhere, gaining the recognition of religiously-minded philanthropists. Many enlightened *'ulamā'* support these organizations and encourage wealthy people to pay their *zakāt* to them.

The Islamic awakening, which has been influencing Muslim societies during the last two decades has touched off a crucial and heated debate among the Islamists about the best way of *da'wah* in order to establish an Islamic society. Three major trends may be noted among various Islamic groups: the violent way, followed by *jihād* groups in Egypt and recently in Algeria; the political method, followed by Jama'ti Islami in Pakistan and the Muslim Brotherhood in Egypt; and the educational way, practised by Sufi orders and Jamā'at al-Tabliqh. Local and international conditions will play a major role in determining which trend will prevail in the decades to come. In general, when Islamist groups are recognized as legitimate parties and governments respect civil liberties, the inclination to use violent methods is weakened or made redundant. The *'ulamā'* who should have influenced young men towards moderation and peaceful means had discredited themselves by always taking the side of governments.

Social functions

The oldest social institutions in Islam are *zakāt* and *awqāf* (endowment). *Awqāf* has been under the ministry of religious affairs in many countries since the 1950s. Turkey was the first country to nationalize the *awqāf* in the early 1920s, followed by Egypt in the 1950s. The previous arrangement was to give the donor the right to appoint a person or committee to administer the *waqf* as a trust according to the conditions he set. With the passage of time, the change of persons and committees and lack of proper official supervision, this arrangement did not prove to be satisfactory. However, putting it completely under a government department has meant that *awqāf* properties are suffering from misuse of funds, cheap investment and confiscation of lands to sell them or use them for government purposes. Use of *waqf* funds for any purpose other than the original one stated by the donor and sale of *waqf* property are strictly prohibited in Islam, for the *waqf* is supposed to be a permanent trust.

In countries like Saudi Arabia and Yemen, where courts abide by *Sharī'ah* rulings, it is possible for the beneficiaries to win a case against government misuse of *waqf*. Perhaps a more effective arrangement is to have a *waqf* council, constituted from distinguished personalities, businessmen and *'ulamā'* who are known to be of good character, under the chairmanship of the minister for religious affairs. Nevertheless, *Sharī'ah* courts should be the final arbitration authority in the case of dispute with beneficiaries.

The collection and distribution of *zakāt* is voluntary in most Muslim countries, though in recent years it has become an obligatory tax in Sudan and Pakistan and it has always been obligatory in North Yemen. In Iran it is the prerogative of *'ulamā'* to collect *zakāt*, which is eight times that of Sunnīs, and to distribute it to poor people and to religious institutions. Sudan has expanded the traditional sources of *zakāt* — agricultural producc, cattle and trade — to cover all kinds of income, and efficient government collection has made this a substantial source of finance. An administration is set in each province under a supreme *zakāt* council, which includes *'ulamā'*, businessmen and public personalities and is headed by a judge of a high *Sharī'ah* court. A network of public committees all over the country selects the poor families deserving of *zakāt*.

This Sudanese experiment has proved that the institution of *zakāt* can have a tremendous social impact if it is taken seriously and is well-administered.

Wedding ceremonies may be performed by any Muslim, but for the sake of official registration, the ministry for religious affairs assigns persons of reasonable religious knowledge to administer the marriage contract. Although the contract is valid if performed by any Muslim, it has to be registered with local authority through those officially assigned. Some people, especially in rural areas, choose to contract marriages in the mosque, which makes the ceremony simpler and far less expensive.

The judiciary

Theoretically the entire legal system of a Muslim country should be based on *Sharī'ah*, the code of law in Muslim countries for many centuries. Due to the rigidity of *'ulamā'* and general stagnation in society, the Ottoman caliphate in its last decades began to adopt some European laws. The break from tradition occurred after European colonization of the Muslim world in the 19th century. Not only were European laws imposed to replace the *Sharī'ah*, but European judges and languages dominated the courts of most Muslim countries. The *Sharī'ah* was left to administer only the family law.

This situation has continued, more or less, in most Muslim countries up to this day. However, the call for the implementation of *Sharī'ah* in all spheres of life, especially in courts of law, has never been abandoned since the achievement of independence after the second world war.

The contemporary Islamic awakening has made this a burning issue as never before. Countries such as Iran, Pakistan and Sudan have started to Islamize their laws; North Yemen and Saudi Arabia have based their legal system on *Sharī'ah* for many decades.

The experience of codifying *Sharī'ah* has raised several problems. Its non-application for several decades created a gap, especially in the economic sector, between Islamic theory and real society. Traditional *'ulamā'* are not competent to bridge this gap, as their training is remote from the real problems of society. Professional judges and economists who have acquired Islamic knowledge may be of greater help in solving these problems than ordinary *'ulamā'*, since it is easier to convey to these professionals the basic principles of Islam concerning a given problem than to convey the necessary knowledge of economy or law to the religious scholar.

The trend in Iran, Sudan and Pakistan is to combine *'ulamā'* and experts in the membership of supervisory bodies in order to ensure that laws and decisions are in conformity with the *Sharī'ah*. Iran has the Guardianship Council to veto any legislation that contravenes Islam. Sudan established the Supreme Organization for Islamic Supervision over Banks and Financial Institutions, which may decide against any transaction that is not sanctioned by Islam. Pakistan created a Federal *Sharī'ah* Court to rule against non-Islamic laws and decisions; however, its decisions may be overruled by the Supreme Court.

Experience also shows that most civil and criminal laws adapted from European sources are not necessarily repugnant to the Qur'ān and Sunnah. As the objective of *Sharī'ah* is the *maṣlaḥah* (public good), such laws may be enacted in any Islamic code. As a matter of fact most of the controversy about Islamic laws concerns the prohibition of *ribā* (interest) and intoxicants, and the prescribed punishments for apostasy, theft and fornication.

Training judges for the implementation of Islamic laws in all fields is another area requiring a new approach. The old approach must benefit from Western training in faculties of law.

Fatwā

This is an old Islamic tradition which is closely associated with *'ulamā'*. The office of grand *muftī* was known in the Ottoman caliphate. He gave the religious opinions in response to queries from individuals or to questions from the government on public affairs. The present tendency is to form an *iftā'* council, made up of a number of prominent *'ulamā'*, as is the case in Sudan, Saudi Arabia and Pakistan. Many people are suspicious of government appointees, and they seek *fatwā* in personal matters from *'ulamā'* they trust. Journals and radio programmes usually seek answers to religious queries from popular *'ulamā'* without much attention to any official designation. An *iftā'* council is more likely to withstand pressure from the government than an individual *muftī*. In Egypt the official High Council for Islamic Research recently dared to issue a *fatwā* about *ribā* contradicting the one given by the Grand Mufti under governmental pressure. Furthermore, such a council could include experts in useful fields of specialization.

* * *

Hence, we may conclude that there is no significant official role for the *'ulamā'*. Their contribution depends mainly upon their persuasive influence on society. However, there is room for effective religious institutions in the areas of spiritual rites, missionary work, education, social work, judiciary and *iftā'*. Although *'ulamā'* are needed to guide these institutions according to the teachings of Qur'ān and Sunnah, this is by no means confined to them. Religious opinion derives its strength from its logical validity based on Qur'ān and Sunnah rather than from a person or an office. The common man who cannot assess the logical validity of an opinion goes by the trust he has for a special scholar. This is why imāms of the four known Sunnī schools of thought managed to spread their *Madhāhib* all over the world despite opposition from the caliphs of their times.

Part V

16. Human Rights and Islamic Revivalism

WALID SAIF

Suddenly the world seems to have discovered a great human cause to struggle for. The world community and the Western powers in the North seem to acknowledge the consistent violations of human rights in the so-called third world in the South. An old enemy is gone, but a new one is emerging, creating a new opportunity for the good, the beautiful and the brave to continue their mission of tracking down and casting out the spirit of evil in a battered world. One needs a villain to make a hero; and it is no coincidence that the emergence of human rights discourse in the international arena has come after the collapse of the former Soviet Union and the communist regimes and along with a worldwide obsession with what is called Islamic fundamentalism, extremism and militant violent groups.

An association — sometimes implicit, often explicit — is created between the human rights issue and the postulated danger of Islamic fundamentalism. The approach of Western mass media is first to create an association between the human rights issue and Islamic militant groups, then to extend this to the whole Muslim world and thereafter to insinuate that Islam and its culture are essentially and inherently inimical to human rights (as defined in Western discourse and projected as having a universal validity and international value). In effect Islam is depicted as essentially a religion of violence, extremism and absolutism.

Following this line of propaganda, the victims of gross human rights violations in the Arab world and Muslim countries paradoxically end up being portrayed as the victimizers — a potential danger if not an actual threat to humanity and world peace. Instead of state oppression and violence in the Arab and Muslim world, the focus is on what is called Islamic fundamentalism, which is associated with violence that threatens the whole world order and thus calls for concerted national and international efforts to stop it for the sake of human rights.

The nature of Islamic revival

All this obscures issues and ignores facts. The distortion begins with the misleading term "Islamic fundamentalism". Although the Arabic media have widely adopted the term in its Arabic translation *uṣuliyyah*, it immediately stirs negative reactions and resentment among most Islamists and Muslim adherents, including enlightened intellectuals. The common feeling is that the term has been imposed by the dominant Western media and makes an implicit political statement. Borrowed from Western cultural and conceptual terminology, it reflects a different socio-cultural and historical context and therefore denotes a concept that is not applicable in the Arabic-Islamic context. Moreover, the term has negative connotations in Western culture itself, thus reflecting immediately a negative value judgment. Many Muslims see the adoption of the term by the Arabic media as one more example of a common trend of alienation and Westernization in Arab and Muslim societies as a result of Western cultural and political domination.

In addition, using the term to describe indiscriminately all Islamic trends and movements perpetuates a common reductionist misconception that Islamic revival trends form a single homogeneous and coherent phenomenon, which is in turn associated with extremism and militancy, thus justifying the search for simple generalizations, abstractions and stereotypes. In reality, the Islamic movement includes a wide spectrum of divergent organizations, groups and trends, including a great number of independent individuals, thinkers and intellectuals who are not affiliated with any specific organized body. On certain points and aims they converge; but on other important conceptions, aims, attitudes and perspectives they diverge, sometimes sharply.

In terms of both conceptual content and methods and means, they range from the militant extremist to the most moderate and enlightened. And although they all appeal to the same major religious resources, mainly Qur'ān and Sunnah, and all share a set of common values and goals, they nevertheless make different interpretations, represent various attitudes and stands concerning several major issues (such as democracy and the role and status of women) and adopt different methods and means.

In some cases, it is even difficult to identify one specific movement with a single coherent, integral mode of thought. Heterogeneity and diversity of perspectives and trends may be found within the same movement or party. Sometimes outside observers conceive of the so-called Islamic fundamentalist groups as essentially fanatic religious organizations, in the sense that their main motivations and objectives are to impose strict religiously prescribed moral standards on people, often using violent means. At other times they are projected by unsympathetic media as merely exploiting religious sentiments to achieve political power for self-interest. Such conceptions overlook the fact that the Islamic movement is not merely an ideological stream developing in an abstract and independent history of thought. Rather, it is a social movement, conditioned by social, economic and political circumstances. An adequate understanding should not overlook the relation between this movement and the common search for national identity. Its public base cuts across all sectors of society, especially the lower classes, and draws on deeply rooted religious sentiments and values. Thus it cannot be reduced to stereotypes projected by prejudiced media.

Although militant and violent Islamic groups act outside the Islamic mainstream, and while we all reject and denounce extremism, militancy, intolerance and the use of violent means for political ends, we should not ignore the role played by dictatorship, state oppression, lack of institutional democracy, absence of social justice, failure of alien models of development insensitive to national culture and Western domination in creating a suitable atmosphere for the emergence of frustrated militant extremist groups acting outside the main Islamic stream. Violence is bound to breed violence.

Viewed as being motivated by both socio-economic and political conditions on the one hand and by the principles of Islam and *Sharī'ah* on the other, the Islamic revival movement, although heterogeneous in reality, shares a set of common goals and objectives which can be summed up briefly and generally as follows:

1. Application of *Sharī'ah* rules, principles and values in Muslim societies and their public institutions.
2. Development of a socio-economic and political system reflecting Islamic principles and *Sharī'ah*.
3. Promotion of cultural identity based on Islamic principles and heritage, which would signify historical continuity and represent a defensive response to alienation associated with Western cultural domination.
4. Promotion of Islamic moral values in everyday behaviour and social interactions at both the individual and the collective levels.
5. Production of a socio-economic model of development free from and independent of the Western industrial centre, which is sensitive to national culture and responds to actual local needs. This model stems

from the historical and objective conditions of Arab and Muslim societies.

6. Promotion of Arabic unity as a pre-condition for a wider Islamic unity, based on the shared history of Islamic values, *Sharī'ah* principles and common interests.
7. Revival of Islamic civilization as a model with a universal message so that the Arab and the Muslim world may restore its international status.

These very general objectives and aims should not mislead us into overlooking the significant differences in conceptual methods and means to achieve those aims, as in other theoretical aspects, concepts and attitudes concerning more specific issues, such as the meanings and practical implications of *Sharī'ah*, attitudes towards the *fiqh* heritage and how much of it has been historically conditioned, attitudes towards *ijtihād* and who is to exercise it and how, the status and role of women, democracy and pluralism, socio-economic development and modernization, relations with the West and with an increasingly interdependent world.

Regarding means we may distinguish three general models:

1. The *reformist moderate* model advocates the use of peaceful means to produce the desired change. The stress here is on evolution rather than revolution or radical change. One of the basic common ideas is to build up a general public awareness and opinion and to create a wide public base through such means as education, guidance, preaching (*da'wah*) and the establishment of effective Islamically oriented service and public institutions. Creating such a broad base in public opinion by drawing on deep Islamic values and historical roots would pressure governments to respond positively and practically to the general public demand and thus to move towards the application of *Sharī'ah* and other Islamic goals. Within the general framework of this model there is now a growing acceptance of and even demand for the introduction of a democratic process which would enable the Islamic movement to participate in the institution of a political system and therefore influence political and strategic decision-making towards Islamic goals relying on the wide Islamic public base.

This reformist moderate model represents the mainstream, including a large number of independent individuals, thinkers and intellectuals.

2. Adherents of the *revolutionary militant* model believe that the current oppressive regimes are dictated by their foreign, Western masters, that they represent illegitimate dictatorships and even if they were to

establish some sort of democracy it would be a counterfeit one, tailored to preserve their power and serve their own interests and those of their masters. Only revolution can bring about an Islamic state and the sought-after change which reflects the will and choice of the majority. This model cannot be identified with one single group or central leadership.

3. The *military camp* model is adopted in particular by the Al-taḥrir party.

The aforementioned models of means and methods are given in very broad terms. However, it should be mentioned that the adoption of moderate peaceful means does not always ensure conceptual moderation, intellectuality and enlightenment in attitudes concerning major specific issues. There is growing debate within the mainstream itself between more rigid and traditional perspectives on the one hand and broader and more modern points of view on the other. For instance, there is a growing awareness that the Islamic movement should go beyond vague ideological slogans and abstractions to propose practical solutions and programmes, dealing realistically with regional and institutional conditions, on specific issues. This is mainly advocated by enlightened intellectuals and thinkers, independent and otherwise, who maintain a broader perspective of the desirable change.

On this view the change required is not confined to the promotion of Islamic moral values and the formal application of *Sharī'ah* in and by the political system. Islam should be the driving force for modernity, development and renaissance in all their material, social, political, cultural, technological, scientific and spiritual manifestations. The Islamic project should draw on the principles of Islam and the purpose of *Sharī'ah* (*maqāṣid al-sharī'ah*) to produce a modern model of progress and civilization which reflects its universal values. This is essentially an historical process which can be achieved by enlightenment, active participation in world affairs, production of knowledge and accumulation of progress at all levels of social life. It reflects a comprehensive development process which stems from the historical context and the objective circumstances of the Arab and Muslim societies and which responds to prevailing needs and political challenges without isolating itself from other cultures and world experiences. Its components are mutually interdependent and mutually conditioned, including cultural, social, economic, educational and political development. The required Islamic society is not merely one which observes Islamic principles and *Sharī'ah* values while remaining underdeveloped and backward. Such a state can only frustrate the common value of Islam and will lack credibility.

Islam and human rights

I have gone into some detail here in trying to draw a very general picture of Islamic trends, highlighting their diversity and their grassroots character in the prevailing social, economic, cultural and political context in order to encourage a better understanding of Islamic revivalism over against the prevailing misconceptions which reduce it to a mere fanatic movement that threatens human rights. Worse than that is the tendency to extend this presumption about the so-called Islamic fundamentalism to the whole of Muslim society and thereafter to the Islamic framework in general, implying that extremism is inherent and latent in it.

It is extremely dangerous to pose Islam as the new enemy of world peace. Such discourse cannot serve the promotion of human rights in the world in general and in the Arab and Muslim world in particular. It gives moral support, justification and legitimation for more state oppression and violence, which can only result in more violations of human rights on the part of the state and elicit more militancy in response. It also weakens the position of the more moderate enlightened Muslim intellectuals in the growing debate within the Islamic scene itself.

Undoubtedly the Muslim world has long suffered from persistent violations of human rights and lack of democracy. But this call for promoting human rights loses much of its credibility and defeats its own claims by creating such images of Islam. The growing common feeling is that the recent rise of human rights discourse in relation to the Muslim world is meant to conceal the coercion which lies behind it: that what is actually taking place is an attempt to construct a moral discourse to justify intervention and domination in much the same way as classical colonialism justified itself by such concepts as extending enlightenment, progress, modernity and education to "primitive" societies.

If there is really a sincere interest in introducing and promoting democracy and human rights in the Arab world and Muslim world, and if efforts in this direction are to be fruitful, those values should not be alienated from the broad Islamic perspective. The way they are presented should not hint that the question is essentially and particularly problematic in the Islamic context. In other words, people in the Arab and Muslim world should not be driven to the point of having only two mutually exclusive alternatives: either Islam (and hence their national cultural identities) or human rights. If so, the first loser will be human rights themselves. Human rights discourse should not be presented as a Western invention, with the West assuming the role of the global custodian of human rights, so that people in our part of the world are made to identify the issue with Westernization, cultural alienation and foreign intervention. In that case, many of the victims of human rights violations in our societies will be inclined either to resent the whole issue or at least remain passive. We do not want to face a new situation similar to that in which the concept of modernity came to be identified with secularism and Westernization, thus stirring up a defensive response of resentment and resulting in a destructive polarization between cultural enclosure and retreat to a past model on the one hand and Westernization in the name of progress and modernity on the other.

Human rights discourse should not be used as yet another tool for the Americanization of world culture or to divert our attention from other less publicized domains of human rights which have been subject to constant violation by those who now pose themselves as the guardians of human rights.

Surely many regimes in Arab and Muslim countries that have long abused human rights and denied their people the right to participate in the political process have been set up and supported by Western powers, notably the United States. And surely human rights are not confined to individual liberties. If these are to be realized, due attention should be paid to the structural foundations and objective pre-conditions, including socio-economic factors, for human rights. Human rights also apply in relations between nations. Ignoring the right of a whole nation to self-determination is a gross violation of human rights. Double-standard international politics, the widening gap between rich and poor countries, exhaustion of natural resources to feed an ever-greedy capitalist machine, the growing concentration of wealth, the destruction of the environment to the point of threatening the future of life on our planet — all work against human rights and question the credibility of the call for human rights by major international powers. These are areas of human rights often ignored, thus reinforcing a common and growing feeling that the whole issue of human rights is now being constructed to divert our attention away from these areas, for which the major powers take responsibility, to the areas for which Arab and Muslim countries are to take responsibility.

Of course, this is not to say that we need not respond to the issue of human rights positively and actively. On the contrary, the situation sketched above should drive us to try to strike a balance and to put things in perspective. Both Muslims and Christians are called to engage in a constructive dialogue on the subject, drawing on their universal spiritual and humanistic resources, thus contributing to the formulation of the discourse instead of reacting defensively to the current situation and the political coercion which may be behind it. The one who exclusively owns the discourse owns the power, but scepticism in response to the powers which now claim the discourse does not and should not conceal the fact that the current situation in the Arab and Muslim world is far from being in line with human rights. We must also acknowledge the fears that many of the opposition political movements, including the Islamic movement, are not very promising in terms of human rights should they come to power. For example, some maintain — and surely this is what the official media often voice — that the Islamic movement is not really sincere in its declared acceptance of the principle of democracy and pluralism, that it has a hidden agenda to use democracy as a temporary tool for gaining power only to discard it afterwards and establish a totalitarian system. There are also understandable fears that an envisaged Muslim state observing *Sharī'ah* would undermine the status and rights of other non-Muslim minorities.

The need for dialogue

These are some of the issues which Muslims and Islamists should address openly, specifically and without equivocation. And this would open a dialogue not only between Islamists and other parties but also and perhaps more significantly within the Islamic movement itself. Although Islamists might maintain that Islam ensures human rights and equality among all citizens irrespective of religion, race or gender, I believe more has to be done both to address specific issues and to formulate them in a working institutional framework in an envisaged Muslim state, lest they remain vague theoretical slogans. One must realistically admit that some of the basic and specific issues are still subject to debate among Islamists, reflecting a "traditional" vs. "modern" division which in turn shows that a great deal of interpretation is involved in the issue. Differences in interpretations may in part be linked to the differences in attitudes towards the *fiqh* heritage, *Sharī'ah* and history and their relationships. Does the accumulated *fiqh* heritage have an absolute truth value that transcends time and place or is it, at least in part, historically conditioned? Does Islamic revivalism mean the reproduction of past historical models or the production of a modern model that complies with the ultimate purposes of *Sharī'ah* and responds creatively to current conditions?

In my essay on "*Sharī'ah* and Modernity" (pp.11-19), I noted that I accept the view that at least a large part of the inherited *fiqh* corpus has to be situated in its historical context; that this was voiced clearly by the great *fuqahā'* themselves: "the changing of rulers along with the change of time"; that *maqāṣid al-sharī'ah* are the guidelines and the principles against which rules of *fiqh* are to be measured for validity; that the vitality of Islam lies in the ability to produce new models in response to changing times and places; that a distinction has to be maintained between historical models which essentially are the product of interaction between Islamic framework, human activity and objective circumstances and the *Sharī'ah* frame of reference.

Muslim history has not always complied with the principles of Islam. This certainly applies to the issue of human rights. For example, I believe that the status of women has changed in the course of Muslim history under the influence of a male-dominated society and culture. This has not only influenced *fiqh* in different ways, but also led many Muslims to confuse some inherited traditional cultural values with Islamic values. Fortunately, an *'alim* whose knowledge of *fiqh* and adherence to Islam are not questioned, 'Abd al-Ḥalim Abu Shiqqah' has recently published a volume on the subject of women in the time of the Prophet in which he tries to sort out the historical ambiguities and to give what seems to be a new perspective, although it is all based on Qur'ān and documented Sunnah.

This work marks a growing awareness among enlightened revisionist *'ulamā* and intellectuals of the need to take up anew some issues which long seemed outside the Islamic critical gaze. The subject of the status of non-Muslims in an Islamic state and within *Sharī'ah* is another major issue which needs to be addressed by Muslims and Islamic activists in open and specific terms. Once again we have to differentiate between historical experience and the Islamic theoretical framework.

The fears and scepticism associated with this issue are understandable and legitimate. Failure to address them and to give clear answers can only open the door for foreign powers to manipulate and amplify fears for their own interests, resulting in reciprocated doubts and distrust.

To my mind, even to discuss the subject under the label "rights of non-Muslims" is misleading and probably counterproductive, because it may imply that non-Muslims in an Islamic state are singled out as being a special category with a somehow different status. It is not enough — and I speak as an adherent Muslim — to cite historical instances of Islamic tolerance or to make reassuring comparisons between the way Christians have been treated through most of the Islamic history and the way Muslim minorities have often been mistreated and abused in non-Muslim societies. Comparison with bad examples is the worst frame of reference, because it creates unconstructive complacency.

Yet, regardless of Muslim historical experience, which has been mostly characterized by tolerance, mutual respect, understanding, co-existence and interaction, I may say with all sincerity that I know nothing in *Sharīʻah* based on Qur'ān and documented Sunnah that undermines the total equality of Muslim and Christian citizens in a Muslim state in terms of both rights and responsibilities, except where a responsibility is deemed an act of religious worship, so that imposing it would amount to religious coercion, which is itself a violation of a major human right, namely freedom of religion. Muslims have the responsibility to make it absolutely clear that *maqāṣid al-sharīʻah* ensures equality, and that any ruling or act that undermines this principle is contradictory to *Sharīʻah*.

There is not space here for a fully detailed account of the *Sharīʻah* stand regarding the rights of and equality for People of the Book. I would however point out that focussing on the question of the rights of non-Muslim minorities in Muslim historical experience often creates the illusion that the rights of the Muslim majority can be taken for granted, that the division on human rights is between Muslim and non-Muslim. This is far from the truth. In reality, the division has mostly been between oppressive totalitarian regimes together with the social forces they represented and the public at large, including sincere independent *'ulamā'*. Most of the violent sectarian and political conflicts have been between Muslim groups, parties and sects, or between the official authorities and the masses. History even records instances in which Muslim individuals had to pretend they were Christians in order to escape death at the hands of their Muslim captors, the rationale being: the *dhimmi* is protected by *Sharīʻah*, his religion is recognized and acknowledged and thus his right to religious freedom is ensured, whereas punishment of a Muslim deemed heretic or *murtadd* or accused of stirring *fitnah* (threatening social order) is religiously legitimate from the standpoint of his adversary. Of course, these labels and categories were often the product of politically motivated interpretations.

The term *dhimmi* has come to have negative connotations among Christians in Arab and Muslim societies, although it was not so when it was first coined and used. Originally it was meant to emphasize and safeguard their rights in a Muslim state with a Muslim majority, so that any violation of those rights is considered to be directed against God and his Prophet. Now the term is associated with fears that it creates a special category which may signify a second-class citizenship. I strongly believe, as many Muslim intellectuals agree, that the term in itself has no constant *Sharīʻah* value, and if it offends Christians it can and should be discarded.

Fortunately, many Muslim thinkers and activists are now responding positively to the question of human rights, trying to produce an Islamic version with a universal human dimension, thus accommodating that in their Islamic socio-political project. A number of books have been published in this respect, and some organized bodies have been set up. I may refer here to the work of Rāshid al Ghannūnshī on "Liberties in Islam" and "The Rights of Minorities in Islam" and to the International Committee for Human Rights formed by a number of *'ulamā'* and thinkers, supervised and headed by Salīm 'Azzām. This committee has produced a document on human rights from an Islamic perspective, which was adopted in its entirely by the International Islamic Conference on Human Rights based in Khartoum.

A major issue to be addressed in the context of human rights is the problematic one of universality and cultural relativity. What can be accepted as a universal value, justifying international obligation, and what is to be considered relative, bound to local cultures whose respect also lies in the area of human rights? How should we react to a certain concept stated in the United Nations' Universal Declaration of Human Rights if that concept contradicts a local cultural value, including *Sharī'ah* rulings?

Obviously the situation is potentially dangerous at both ends. On the one hand, a claim to universality and international obligation may be manipulated by international powers as a pretext for intervention to serve self-interests and political ends. We have already witnessed examples of double-standard politics. On the other hand, dictatorships and oppressive regimes may equally manipulate the concept of cultural relativity to justify continuation of oppression and abuse of human rights.

I shall not here attempt to outline a solution to this, but only suggest that here institutional democracy can play a crucial role in striking the balance — democracy as both an essential part of human rights and as a prerequisite for other rights such as free choice and freedom of religion. It is possible that in practice we may find that the imposition of a certain right clashes with another basic one, such as the right of peoples to preserve and promote their own cultures, freedom of religion and freedom of choice through democracy.

Democracy, pluralism and public participation can serve to lift both the pressure of international powers under the pretext of protecting universally prescribed human rights, and the pressure of local oppressive regimes under the pretext of conforming to local culture and traditions. After all, free choice is at the core of human rights and may be viewed as the essence of all facets of human rights, and therefore it should supersede any other claim by the self-declared "big brothers", whether national or international. Democracy would also help to demolish the structural foundation of political militancy on the part of the opposition as a negative response to state oppression, corruption and denial of democratic participation.

I would like to conclude with the following remark. It is very misleading to identify militancy and radicalism with the Islamic movement in the context of the division Islamic vs. secular. Moderate and radical trends cut across different ideologies and political movements. After all, official abuse of human rights in the Arab and Muslim world has long been practised mostly by states which are basically secular.

Part V

17. Differing Perceptions of Human Rights

Asian-African Interventions at the Human Rights Conference

THOMAS MICHEL

The United Nations Human Rights Conference in Vienna in June 1993 provided a forum for airing contrasting perspectives on questions of human rights. During the debates which took place in the course of two weeks, five areas of controversy emerged which have a bearing on the understanding of human rights.[1]

Are human rights universal?

The most fundamental controversy arose over the question of the universality of human rights. Do human rights derive from the very nature and dignity of the human person, so that they are identical all over the world? Or should they be viewed as culturally relative — that is, that one culture may accept that a person has a certain right but that right might properly be denied in another culture?

Acceptance or rejection of the principle of the universality of human rights has sweeping implications, both within nations and internationally. Deep convictions and intense emotions surround the issue, and battle-lines were already drawn before the conference. All delegations were prepared for a heated debate. In his opening address UN secretary general Boutros Boutros Ghali insisted that universality is of the essence of human rights and suggested that the acceptance of this principle was one of three imperative priorities of the conference: "universality, guarantees and democratization".

The US delegation quickly expressed a view shared by most Western European countries: there must be a single standard of behaviour everywhere in the world. Rights are not relative to particular cultures. "We cannot allow cultural relativism to become the last refuge of repression," the US delegate stated. A diametrically opposed view was presented by the People's Republic of China: no rights inhere in persons other than those accorded them by the state. In other words, human rights are by their nature solely and properly an internal affair of the state. If human rights find their basis in the relationship of the individual to the state, it follows that it is an arrogant violation of a country's sovereignty for another nation to accuse it of human rights abuses.

Asked to comment on the view expressed by the Chinese delegation, the Dalai Lama said most Asians do not agree with China's analysis of rights. All humans want freedom, equality and dignity, he affirmed, irrespective of what rights might be granted by governments. Even if human rights are not universally respected in practice, human hopes and aspirations are the same everywhere. The Holy See, which took part in the conference as an official observer, held that human rights are not culturally determined, but belong to the dignity bestowed on all people by the Creator. The position of Muslim delegates on the issue was mixed. The general view was that human rights do not arise from the nature of the human person, but are rather granted to humans by the Creator.

Some delegations from predominantly Muslim countries endorsed the principle of the universality of human rights. Turkey, for example, held that it was essential to create a universal human rights system that would encompass all people. However, of the fifteen countries which questioned in one way or another the universality of human rights (China, Colombia, Cuba, India, Indonesia, Iran, Iraq, Libya, Malaysia, Mexico, Myanmar, Pakistan, Sudan, Syria, Yemen) nine were predominantly Muslim nations. No Muslim delegation went so far as to agree with the Chinese position that human rights are simply the civil rights which a state accords its citizens. The Sudanese delegation (headed by a Christian, Anglican Bishop Gabriel Roric) held that human rights are universal and indivisible. However, universality does not imply the denial of cultural specificity.

The Libyan delegation felt that the concept of the universality of human rights, as expressed in United Nations declarations and documents, is unacceptably tied to a Western cultural and philosophical tradition. If there is ever to be any universal agreement on questions of human rights, the principle must be detached from any particular region or system. The Libyan delegation noted that Islamic culture prefers to speak of "human dignity" and Islamic history offers many examples of the importance attached to dignity of the individual.

Some delegations saw a hidden agenda in the assertion of human rights as universal. The spokesman for the Sierra Leone delegation said it would be unfortunate and unfair if the Vienna conference were used as means to pressure developing countries into accepting Western ideals of human rights. As the conference progressed, this view was variously expressed by other delegations.

Do individual or communal rights have any priority over each other?

Many Asian and African countries complained that human rights doctrine is the product of individualist Western society and is not well adapted to collective social traditions elsewhere. On this question, as in many to follow, the Malaysian delegation articulated well the views of others. The Malaysian spokesman averred that Western countries emphasize individual rights at the expense of the community. Excessive individual freedom has led to moral decay and has torn at the fabric of society. In the name of human rights, new forms of racism are arising. Civil and political rights cannot be treated as separate issues but must be developed in tandem with economic, social and cultural rights.

The delegation of the Holy See took up the complex issue of the right to self-determination. On the one hand, acceptance of this principle without nuance could result in a new nationalism, affecting the lives and survival of millions of people. On the other hand, governments must stop abusing their national sovereignty by claiming that human and civil rights are purely internal affairs on which no one else has any prerogative to speak. Representatives of nations must try to come to an agreement on international responsibility for dealing with human rights violations and draw up binding norms determining when and what kinds of intervention from outside are permissible when norms are being violated.

A similar view was put forth by the delegation from Tajikistan. Human rights, it was proposed, go beyond the competence of individual states. Governments that commit massive violations should be brought to an international forum of justice. However, a one-sided accusatory, self-righteous approach to human rights, too often heard in international forums, should give way to a process of dialogue.

Several African delegations stressed that the agenda of poor nations is not the same as that of prosperous countries. The representative of Niger held that, at the global level, the right to development and the alleviation of poverty were the most important issues to be tackled. This was seconded by the Ethiopian speaker, who noted that the right to potable water is as much a right as freedom of expression. The point was that societal rights to a basic minimum of human dignity are more fundamental than the "luxuries" of rights such as the free public expression of views, social and political assembly, dissent and alternative life-styles.

Should development assistance be conditional on observing human rights?

Some civil rights activists proposed that the threat to withdraw development assistance would be an effective measure to put pressure on third world governments to respect the human rights of their citizens. These proponents were joined by some NGOs and minority and revolutionary movements who are militantly and even militarily opposed to various governments. Such suggestions were usually bitterly resented by governments who relied upon international development assistance.

Again, the Malaysia delegation articulated the argument of those who opposed a strategic link between a good human rights record and obtaining development assistance. They argued that linking development assistance to human rights would in fact undermine the protection of those rights. It is only through development at all levels — educational, medical, social, economic, civic and political — that conditions can be created in which democratic institutions can reasonably be expected to flourish. Hindering this development by withholding assistance will have the negative result of condemning populations to continue to suffer violation of their human rights. The Mali delegation arrived at the same principle by a similar logic, claiming that progress in human rights must be accompanied by improvement in economic and social development. To the extent that people are left in poverty without education or health care, human rights is an empty issue.

The League of Arab States concurred, affirming that human rights must not be used as a tactic or pretext to interfere in internal affairs of states. The principle is too vague and opens the door to political manipulation. The League called for a complete separation between political and development issues.

Is a double standard used in the imposition of human rights standards?

On this issue the smouldering resentment of many of the third world governments towards the Western bloc came out into the open. The feeling was widespread that human rights is an issue used selectively by "the West" to promote its own interests whenever it suits them. Western governments were accused of employing "civil rights monitoring" as a pressure tactic to interfere, to influence world public opinion and to weaken politically unfriendly regimes.

The Turkish delegation, which had agreed with the European bloc on the question of the universality of human rights, sharply criticized what it considered a selective approach to those rights among European countries. This selective application has led them to harbour terrorist organizations and racist movements on grounds of human rights, while condemning human rights abuses elsewhere. Selective application of human rights, it asserted, is a veiled expression of newly emerging forms of racism. Governments must act to protect foreigners from racist violence and to combat terrorism. Finally, in what became an oft-repeated accusation, evidence of a short-sighted and biased application of human rights doctrine can be seen in the failure of the international community to lift the arms embargo for Bosnia. In the face of genocide taking place there, the people of that country should be enabled to exercise their right to self-defence.

The spokesman from Libya questioned the very nature of the United Nations as an international structure to promote human rights. How can the Security Council examine human rights in a country that has veto power? Are United Nations sanctions against Libya consistent with human rights that uphold freedom of movement and ensure worldwide distribution of medicine and food? The delegation held that the UN had unwittingly involved itself in a campaign to preclude a fair trial for Libyan citizens.

The Sudanese delegation agreed with Libya in questioning whether the United Nations as it stands can be an effective instrument for the promotion of human rights. The disproportionate power of a few countries in the Security Council prevents a just and fair application of rights. Echoing the view expressed by Libya, they asserted that the veto power held by the permanent members prevents cases of human rights from being pursued against them or nations friendly to them. Until the Security Council is democratized and the veto eliminated, the United Nations will not be able to function as an effective instrument for human rights.

Is it a human right not to be the victim of injustice?

If it is a human right of individuals and societies not to be victimized or treated unjustly, then any question of justice is thereby a question of human rights. Human rights would no longer have a clear-cut agenda — as it has traditionally had up to now — but would become synonymous with questions of justice. Many delegations at the conference took this position as a practical working policy, and raised many cases in which they felt that people or states were being treated unjustly.

For example, Afghanistan proposed a war crimes tribunal with jurisdiction over events in the states of the former Yugoslavia and called for international intervention in the name of human rights to stop genocide in Bosnia, Palestine and Kashmir.

The Iraqi delegation claimed that not only individuals and societies but also states have rights. The most basic is the right to be treated fairly in the international forum. They maintained that the blockade against Iraq was a flagrant violation of this right. The issue of the rights of ethnic and religious minorities in Iraq was exploited by the UN in order to incite sectarian strife, destabilize the country and threaten its unity and territorial integrity. Iraq claimed that its rights to self-determination, development, respect for sovereignty, independence and territorial integrity were infringed.

The question of the rights of refugees and expatriates was raised by more than one delegation. Who will speak for those who are no longer under the jurisdiction of a government that can speak on their behalf? The Palestinian observers asked what right could outweigh that of being able to live peacefully in one's own land under the protection of one's own government. Thus, refugees are deprived of the most basic of human rights.

The Malaysian delegation accused the West of hypocrisy in that the widespread prosperity which is a necessary precondition for concern about human rights is itself based on injustice. Human rights are meaningless in an environment of political instability, poverty and deprivation. The West has had an enormous historical advantage, thanks to the plundered resources of colonies, and thus the luxury of honing its democratic institutions.

Benin raised the question of the right to restitution for injustices committed and asked whether the passage of time absolves wrongdoers of guilt. Like many of its neighbour countries, Benin was until the last century victim of one of the most heinous violations of human dignity: enslavement of its inhabitants and international trafficking in their lives. Time has passed and such activities have ceased, yet not one dollar of reparations has ever been offered, much less paid, to the exploited peoples. Meanwhile, new forms of injustice have arisen. Ramparts have been erected to keep starving people out of islands of prosperity. Burdens of debt overwhelm states and prevent economic progress; trade inequalities further condemn whole peoples to poverty.

Speaking on behalf of the Organization of the Islamic Conference, the delegation from Pakistan stated that it was scandalous that nations would be discussing human rights in Vienna, a short distance from Bosnia, but not treating the widespread violation of human rights taking place in that country. They proposed that in the name of human rights the conference issue a declaration on Bosnia. Bosnia should be exempted from the arms embargo. The conference should urge punishment of genocide and condemn the acquisition of territory by force. It should reject the plan to partition Bosnia. It should advocate reconstruction of the country and the return of refugees to their homes.

That this specific issue came to dominate the final days of the conference and the passage of the resolution, over the abstention of most Western European nations, shows the very different perceptions of priorities and modalities of human rights in Asian and African countries from human rights theory as it has developed in the Western philosophical and social tradition.

NOTE

[1] The UN conference was preceded by a large meeting of non-governmental organizations (NGOs), many of whom came to Vienna specifically to protest one or another instance of human rights violations or to take exception to the officially expressed views of their governments. This paper does not deal with the positions taken by the NGOs, but only those of government delegations and official observers, as reported in the official proceedings of the conference.

Contributors

Dr Ghazi Salahuddin Atabani is state minister at the presidency, Republic of the Sudan.

Mr Mokhtar Ihsan Aziz is director of the Islamic World Studies Centre, Valletta, Malta.

Dr Mohammed Ben-Yunusa is professor at Ahmadu Bello University, Zaria, Nigeria.

Dr Bert F. Breiner is co-secretary for interfaith relations at the National Council of the Churches of Christ, New York, USA.

Mr Asghar Ali Engineer is director of the Institute of Islamic Studies, Bombay, India.

Rev. Heinz Klautke is secretary for relations with Islam of the Evangelical Church in Germany, Hanover, Germany.

Dr Sheila McDonough is professor in the department of religion at Concordia University, Montreal, Canada.

Fr Thomas Michel is head of the office for Islam of the Pontifical Council for Interreligious Dialogue, Vatican.

Dr Jørgen S. Nielsen is director of the Centre for the Study of Islam and Christian-Muslim Relations at Selly Oak Colleges, Birmingham, England.

Dr Walid Saif is professor in the faculty of arts at the University of Jordan, Amman.

Rev. Gé Speelman is secretary for Christian-Muslim relations of the Netherlands Reformed Church, Driebergen, Netherlands.

Dr Tayyib Zayn Al-Abdin is professor at the International Islamic University, Islamabad, Pakistan.

Dr Khaled Ziadeh is professor at the Lebanese University, Tripoli, Lebanon.